INTRODUCING
Existentialism

Richard Appignanesi and Oscar Zarate

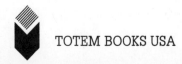

ICON BOOKS UK   TOTEM BOOKS USA

Published in the UK in 2001
by Icon Books Ltd., Grange Road,
Duxford, Cambridge CB2 4QF
E-mail: info@iconbooks.co.uk
www.iconbooks.co.uk

Published in the USA in 2002
by Totem Books
Inquiries to: Icon Books Ltd.,
Grange Road, Duxford,
Cambridge CB2 4QF, UK

Sold in the UK, Europe, South Africa
and Asia by Faber and Faber Ltd.,
3 Queen Square, London WC1N 3AU
or their agents

Distributed to the trade in the USA by
National Book Network Inc.,
4720 Boston Way, Lanham,
Maryland 20706

Distributed in the UK, Europe,
South Africa and Asia by
Macmillan Distribution Ltd.,
Houndmills, Basingstoke RG21 6XS

Distributed in Canada by
Penguin Books Canada,
10 Alcorn Avenue, Suite 300,
Toronto, Ontario M4V 3B2

Published in Australia in 2001
by Allen & Unwin Pty. Ltd.,
PO Box 8500, 83 Alexander Street,
Crows Nest, NSW 2065

ISBN 1 84046 266 3

Reprinted 2002

Printed and bound in Australia
by McPherson's Printing Group, Victoria

A question of absurdity

"There is but one truly serious philosophical problem, and that is suicide. Judging whether life is or is not worth living amounts to answering the fundamental question of philosophy." So begins **Albert Camus** (1913-60) in *The Myth of Sisyphus* (1942). He stiffens the dose by quoting Nietzsche: "a philosopher, to deserve our respect, must preach by example."

But then, Camus at once sees that "a reason for living is also an excellent reason for dying." In either case, a sacrifice might be at stake. The question is – must life have a meaning to be lived? He concludes no, *in view of the absurd*, "it will be lived all the better if it has no meaning."

Into the night and fog

Camus has chosen an "absurdist" estimate of living at a dangerous time, in 1942, in defeated Paris under Nazi Occupation. Others, like himself, are members of the Resistance, an "army of shadows" – men and women who flit unseen in acts of sabotage – always in peril of arrest by the Gestapo, torture and death.

AT ANY STREET CORNER THE FEELING OF ABSURDITY CAN STRIKE ANY MAN IN THE FACE ...

Absurdity, he says, "in its distressing nudity, in its *light without effulgence* ... " Of course, there is a sub-text to Camus' essay on absurdism in this time and place, one which evades the policing of Occupation censorship and is itself an act of defiant resistance.

Absurdity had the evidence of terror. In a fit of Wagnerian megalomania, Hitler issued the *Nacht und Nebel Erlass* – "Night and Fog Decree" – on 7 December 1941, reserved for the inhabitants of the conquered Western territories. It ordered that anyone endangering German security would be seized and made to "vanish without trace into the night and fog of the unknown in Germany." In effect, deportation and death.

As an Irish neutral, I could remain a safe bystander, but I also have a choice ...

The dramatist **Samuel Beckett** (1906-89) in Paris at the time, guaranteed safety by Ireland's neutrality, chose to imperil himself by joining the Resistance. Why? Because to forgo commonsense and accept absurdity in these circumstances is rectitude.

Vichy water into blood

France surrendered to the German invasion after only six weeks' fighting. Without allies – Britain unprepared for war, America neutral, and Hitler now master of Europe – there was no option. On 21 June 1940, **Marshal Philippe Pétain** (1856-1951) signed an armistice which divided France into two zones – one controlled by the Germans, the other "non-occupied", governed from the spa town of Vichy, famous for its curative waters. Political compromise is one thing, quite another was the Vichy government's policy of *active collaboration* with Nazi Germany.

THE VICHY COLLABORATORS SERVE AS HITLER'S HENCHMEN ...

BUT IT WON'T GIVE FRANCE ANY EQUAL FOOTING IN HIS EYES.

Republic of silence

A right-wing element in France seized on the Occupation as the ideal opportunity to adopt Hitler's "Final Solution" for its own unwelcome Jews and Communists – carried out with such zeal that it surprised even the Germans. Vichy transubstantiated the water of political compromise into Nazi blood racialism and with that fed the "shower rooms" of Hitler's concentration camps.

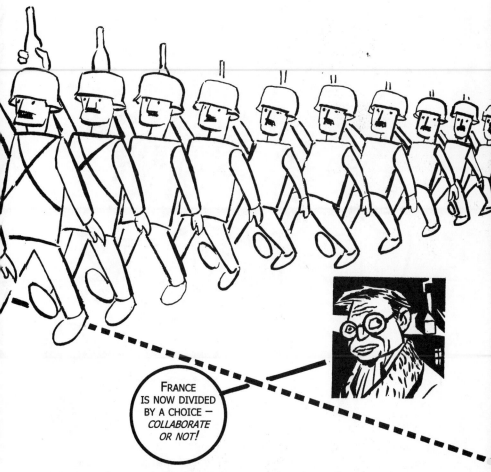

FRANCE IS NOW DIVIDED BY A CHOICE – *COLLABORATE OR NOT!*

Jean-Paul Sartre (1905-80) at this time remarked: "Never have we been freer than under the German Occupation … This total responsibility in total solitude, wasn't this the revelation of our freedom?" (From the essay "La République du silence", 1944.)

Light without effulgence

In such "dark light", does life go on as before? Perhaps one's eyes adjust to reality in the negative. In 1942, **Picasso** (1881-1973) paints his "Still Life with Skull of a Bull", carries on his affair with Dora Maar, and deals in illegal currency. He too enjoys safe neutrality, as a Spanish national, but unlike Beckett does not join the Resistance …

COWARDICE? I CANNOT JUDGE.

NOR CAN I UNDERSTAND WHY THE URBANE, AESTHETICAL DRIEU LA ROCHELLE BECAME A COLLABORATIONIST …

The novelist **Pierre Drieu La Rochelle** (1893-1945) described Occupied Paris as a raped female: "from the central avenue of the Tuileries I can view the Obelisk of Luxor in the Place de la Concorde *piercing* the Arc de Triomphe … " The sexual allusion is fully conscious. Was this reason enough for him to embrace the perspiring masculinity of Nazism?

Bergson's resistance

Nor can I fathom the vile anti-Semitic Collaborationism of such talented novelists as **Louis-Ferdinand Céline** (1894-1961) and **Robert Brasillach** (b. 1909, executed 1945), editor of the sewer-rat fascist paper *Je Suis Partout*. The philosopher **Henri Bergson** (1859-1941) had long foreseen "the formidable wave of anti-Semitism about to break upon the world." Bergson arose mortally ill from his sickbed to register as a Jew in accord with Vichy government law. He refused the exemption offered him.

I AM A JEW AND WOULD RATHER PERISH AS ONE THAN CONCEAL MYSELF.

Is there an image more nauseating than to witness gendarmes of the French Republic and SS troopers "fraternally joined" in the mass deportations of Jews?

Swimming in polluted waters

Paris "after dark" reveals every species of player. Few are actively "Resistants"; most will be *attentistes*, those who literally *wait* to see which side will prevail before choosing between Allies and Nazis. Self-preservation in war-time is indeed a doubtful business, but I can name two at least who chose Resistance – Albert Camus and Jean-Paul Sartre – both so-called Existentialists, if they are in fact really that. They meet in the office of the underground newspaper *Combat* ...

WE SHOOK HANDS IN 1942 – AND BY 1952 WE WERE BITTER ENEMIES ...

... OPPOSED ON THE ISSUES OF MARXISM, THE SOVIET UNION, AND SOON AFTER ON THE QUESTION OF ALGERIAN INDEPENDENCE.

There is an obscure sense of "betrayal" at the heart of Existentialism. Let's consider the case of **Martin Heidegger** (1889-1976), totemic "founder" of Existentialism who utterly disclaimed that role.

How is it with Heidegger?

Karl Löwith (1897-1973), a former student of Heidegger and a refugee Jew in Italy, records their meeting in Rome on 2 April 1936. Heidegger had lectured there on "Hölderlin and the essential nature of poetry". Löwith wondered: what has the Swastika in Heidegger's buttonhole (obviously he doesn't believe it is offensive to me) got to do with Hölderlin's poetry? He then asked the Professor: did his support for Hitler rest on his philosophy? Heidegger agreed it did …

… *seeing it to the end*? After his initial but soon disappointed enthusiasm for Nazism, Heidegger would pretend to "inner emigration", a "flight inwards" to silence, the German equivalent of the *attentiste* waiting and seeing.

For the time being …

Heidegger cannot be held responsible for betraying a "resistant" Existentialism that he never espoused. But a question lingers. Does his philosophy *withstand*, no matter his allegiance? Does history matter to the deepest findings of philosophy that are absolute and universal? In reply, I do know one thing – in the Paris of Camus and Sartre, in the Germany of Heidegger, *I suffocate*. I cannot answer to their conditions. What would I *be*? Would I collaborate, resist, wait? I can only return to the present question …

… *for the time being.* What a miraculous colloquialism, unique to English. What does "time being" mean, lifted out of its everyday commonplace? It is like saying *moment*, but more, a "provisory expectancy". Truly an astonishment to thinking, if I listen deeply to it.

A graveyard of words

Heidegger's armoury is notorious for its teasing, torturing and garrotting of German expressions to arrive at their philological roots and restore primordial freshness to words. The "freshness" of words? What is that?

WORDS ARE BORN AGAIN IN MY MOUTH BY FORGETFULNESS OF THEIR ONCE HAVING BEEN IN OTHERS' ...

I am aware that to write is not only "saying anew" but commemoration. With every step I take as a writer, I proceed on others' graves. The dictionary is a mortuary register but one which strangely inspires rebirths. Hence, precisely as a writer, I must be vigilant to avoid the temptation of literature. What do I mean by that?

What is the attraction of Existentialism?

Could it be that the residue popularity of Existentialism today continues from a legacy of words that still have a power to *scandalize*? Anguish, despair, anxiety, the absurd, authenticity, nothingness, and so on, are literary features that have almost the status of genuine "categories". There is a risk of degrading these existential *feelings* to frivolity, "playing at despair" that Camus so detested. Sartre warns against this in his lecture "Existentialism is a Humanism" (1946).

Literature is therefore a "scandal" impermissible to Existentialism. And yet, did not Sartre write novels and plays, also Camus, and even the redoubtable Heidegger compose verses? In consequence, Existentialism too readily defaults to literature. I am advised to consult Dostoyevsky, Kafka, Beckett – anything but the "austere teaching for technicians".

I would say instead that literature all too obviously appears "existentialist" in retrospective view of that name, and thereby disqualifies itself from the authentication of Existentialism. Consider the term "existential": it is simply an adjective and a logical predicate of *being*. But to affirm or deny that something *is* (as Wittgenstein warned) is a logical proposition of fact that does not "give existence to". Logical usage has no use for an "ism" affixed to "existential".

BUT "EXISTENTIAL" MORE COMMONLY MEANS FOR US "THAT WHICH IS GIVEN TO US TO BE AFFECTED BY" ...

TO BE, OR NOT TO BE, THAT IS THE QUESTION ...

Hamlet's "problem of being" does not of course make him an Existentialist. Besides, he is a fiction, and his speech is Shakespeare's ironic reminder of that. Is this not a clue to disavowing the temptation of literature?

A voice from the dark

Maybe it is not clear yet. I am told, "If you want Existentialism in the raw, go to Dostoyevsky." Very well, I shall. (In this text I do not teach, I *undergo*. To seek authentication is to risk "going under". Humiliation could well be the reward for such study.) I hear a voice like none other, like never before, calling *de profundis*, from the deeps of self-tormenting confession …

Who is this man? A "retired collegiate assessor", some lost soul from a closet in the vast apparatus of Tsarist bureaucracy. No one important. He is a fiction, of course, in *Notes from the Underground* (1846) by **Fyodor Dostoyevsky** (1821-81).

A compelling fiction, only too recognizable. What separates us is merely history – 140 years of more unexplained corpses. I am interested to hear what this "paradoxalist" has to say of his time …

YES, A MAN IN THE 19TH CENTURY MUST AND MORALLY OUGHT TO BE PRE-EMINENTLY A CHARACTERLESS CREATURE …

WHAT · DOES HE MEAN BY "CHARACTERLESS"? IN THE END, HE TELLS US …

"Why, we don't even know what living means now, what it is, and what it is called! Leave us alone without books and we shall be lost and in confusion at once. We shall not know what to join on to, what to cling to, what to love and what to hate, what to respect and what to hate …We are stillborn, and for generations past have been begotten, not by living fathers … . Soon we will contrive to be born somehow *from an idea* … "

The surfeit

Is it clear now? If not, consider this statement by contemporary philosopher **Paul Ricoeur** (b. 1913): "What would we know of love and hatred, of ethical feelings and, in general, of all that we call the Self, if all this had not been brought to language and articulated by literature?" To which the underground man would reply, "But that is exactly my complaint!"

Do I really subscribe to such cultural nihilism? Burn all the books? Or better yet, leave them unread (including this one)? I don't sincerely know. I am still undergoing. "*Sincerely*?", a voice from the dark objects. "Can you ever 'sincerely know' without falling into self-deception?"

Self-deception, bad faith and authenticity

"Nothing is so difficult as not to deceive yourself", Wittgenstein says. But how do I know that I am not? "Bad faith" is a central tenet of Sartre's Existentialism. It is the resource we all have of living in self-deception on the apparent excuse of "not being aware of it". The problem is not one of lying now and then, as we all do, but of *consistent conviction* in self-knowledge. To know I am in *bad faith* implies some conscious degree of *good faith*. But to believe myself in good faith implies a possible deception or even hypocrisy …

Enough! I want to know without "paradoxalism". For this, let me imagine I attend a lecture by Viktor E. Frankl, "Group Psychotherapeutic Experiences in a Concentration Camp" (1951).

Meaning for a "KZler"

"KZler" was a nickname for inmates of Nazi concentration camps. The existential analyst **Viktor Frankl** (1905-1997), himself a KZler, discovered *logotherapy* there. Logotherapy aims to repair a person's sense of meaning (from the Greek, *logos*, reason). The first problem Frankl had to address with KZlers was *entrance-shock*, "a state of panic, accompanied by imminent danger of suicide".

> ANYONE THREATENED WITH "GOING TO THE GAS" MIGHT PREFER "GOING TO THE WIRE" — COMMITTING SUICIDE ON THE HIGH-TENSION WIRES FENCING THE CAMP ...

Frankl somehow organized a team concerned with the prevention of suicides. Isn't that amazing? Why deter suicide when death is an everyday routine of mass killings? Why attempt to "repair meaning" when meaningless existence is a guaranteed condition? "The contrary of suicide is the man condemned to death", says Camus, and that is Frankl's own experience.

Conscious distance from oneself

" … one morning I marched out of camp, scarcely able to endure any longer the hunger, the cold, and the pain in my feet, swollen from oedema, frozen and festering, and stuffed into open shoes. My situation seemed to me to be beyond comfort or hope. Then I imagined to myself that I was standing at a lectern … about to give a lecture entitled 'Group Psychotherapeutic Experiences in a Concentration Camp' … *Believe me, at that moment I could not hope it would ever be granted to me … "*

I PRACTISED SELF-THERAPY, TRYING TO OBJECTIFY MYSELF *AT A DISTANCE* FROM SUFFERING, TO *OUTLIVE THE PRISON.*

Indeed, logotherapy "outlived" the camps and is practicable today, because as Frankl says, "the concentration camp was nothing more than a microcosmic mirroring of the human world as a whole". That lesson applies to "conditions in the world today".

Have the "Night and Fog" truly lifted?

Frankl specifies a pathology of the *now, at present*, which is "marked by provisional, fatalistic, conformist and fanatic attitudes to life which can easily mount to the proportions of a psychic epidemic" of the very kind that symptomized the camps. Frankl's account of his own survival does however raise an existential issue of *willing* self-deception …

YOU ADMIT DECEIVING YOURSELF IN ORDER TO INSPIRE SURVIVAL?

NOT AT ALL. THE ONLY VALID PRECEPT FOR US WAS **FIRST PHILOSOPHIZE, THEN DIE** — TO GIVE AN ACCOUNT TO ONESELF ON THE QUESTION OF ULTIMATE MEANING, AND THEN BE ABLE TO WALK FORTH UPRIGHT AND DIE THE CALLED-FOR MARTYR'S DEATH.

The *dignity* of meaning has final priority, which is to say, we can endure intolerable distance from meaning and retain even *a losing sight of it*. Frankl reverses the commonsense principle – *first live, then philosophize*.

Not surviving is what will happen to us in the end anyway. "The contrary of suicide is the condemned man" – true enough, but for each of them death is maintained in their attitude. (Note: *maintain*, cause to continue, retain in being, support; but also, assert as true.)

I WANT TO *MAINTAIN* FRANKL'S KZLER'S SHOES WHEN I COME TO READ HEIDEGGER'S FAMOUS DISCOURSE ON A PAINTING OF SHOES BY **VINCENT VAN GOGH** (1853-90).

"From the dark opening of the worn insides of the shoes the toilsome tread of the worker stares forth. There is the accumulated tenacity of her slow trudge through the far-spreading furrows of the field swept by a raw wind. On the leather lie the dampness and richness of the soil. Under the soles stretches the loneliness of the field-path as evening falls. In the shoes vibrate the silent call of the earth, its quiet gift of the ripening grain, the fallow desolation of the wintry field."

23

The natural attitude of self-preservation ...

... or the bad habit of living. I am left with Camus' question which of course has its *un*philosophical answer. I can refute suicide by doing as most people do and simply go on living. After all, it is only "a matter of time" anyway. I relapse into *for the time being*, or what the phenomenologist **Edmund Husserl** (1859-1938) addressed as the "natural attitude", which gives philosophy its problems but not solutions. But this already anticipates too much, too soon – better start again with Camus ...

WE GET INTO THE HABIT OF LIVING BEFORE ACQUIRING THE HABIT OF THINKING.

Suicide requires two factors: (1) Realizing the meaningless absurdity of life and then (2) overcoming one's attachment to life (" ... the body shrinks from annihilation"). Suicide usually has a reason "vital" enough to overpower self-preservation – illness, shame and despair.

Metaphysical or "virgin" suicide

"Rarely is suicide committed … through reflection", Camus observes. Can there be a suicide uncontaminated by reasons of deficits (illness, shame etc.), a "logically disposed" one, so to speak, unmotivated by negatives of depression or even paradoxically by fear or death? In short, an entirely *virgin* suicide? Yes, a selfishly metaphysical one of protest? Because it is so rare, Camus resorts to an example from literature …

But does not declaring suicide for "an idea" presuppose a motivation of some sort? What *is* Kirilov's idea?

An absurd syllogism

Absurd reasoning is what drives Kirilov's fatal thought. "I know God is necessary and must exist. I also know that he does not and cannot exist." And this realization alone is sufficient reason to kill oneself. But why should the non-existence of God conclude in *logical* suicide? The premise of Kirilov's absurd syllogism is this: "If God does not exist, I am God." But it is not conclusive simply to *think* oneself God: to *be* God requires that I kill myself. Even in terms of absurd logic, this still isn't clear, until …

... UNTIL I REALIZE THE FREEDOM THAT DIVINITY IS BY BRINGING IT DOWN TO EARTH.

FOR THREE YEARS, I SOUGHT THE ATTRIBUTE OF MY DIVINITY AND I HAVE FOUND IT. THE ATTRIBUTE OF MY DIVINITY IS INDEPENDENCE.

Ending my servitude to immortality means replacing it with "my idea", but also to draw the final consequences of that independence. "Man simply invented God in order not to kill himself", Kirilov states. "That is the summary of universal history down to this moment."

The absurd forbids suicide

Out of love for humanity, then, Kirilov must kill himself to show others the "royal road". It is a *pedagogical* suicide. Of course it is, since it is a lesson demonstrated in a book, first in Dostoyevsky's and next in Camus'. What is their lesson? Dostoyevsky's Christianity forbids suicide; and so does Camus on purely atheistic grounds. Camus arrives at that by *maintaining* absurdity, not denying it or allowing any metaphysical evasions.

THE ABSURD HAS MEANING ONLY INSOFAR AS IT IS NOT AGREED TO.

LIFE HAS NO MEANING. IT IS INESCAPABLY ABSURD. IT ASKS ONLY WHETHER I CAN LIVE WITH IT OR DIE OF IT.

Suicide *settles* the absurd by agreeing to it. Living is experiencing it fully but *without reconciliation*. And that's Camus' point. Not being reconciled to the absurd does not free me of it but will serve to disqualify suicide from genuine absurd experience of living.

The condemned man's reprieve

Camus would like me to live not only "remote from suicide" but "without appeal", that is, in analogy with his condemned man. Fine, but he himself notes something at odds in Kirilov's behaviour: *he performs gymnastics every morning to preserve his health*. At odds with his fatal thought, maybe, but not inconsistent with keeping fit on Death Row. Those sentenced to death do not stop brushing their teeth and, even less surprisingly, invest themselves in appeals for a reprieve.

For us, death is the unexpected that happens *only to others*. Between suspended certainty and the unexpected, there is an abysmal difference of tone, texture and time. And yet, for both of us, the reprieve is *for the time being*.

Is death necessary?

Life is not about its meaning – or only rarely when we're faced with it – but about living *indefinitely*. Note this word's ambiguity: "vague", "undefined"; but also "for *unlimited time*". Let's bring that reprieve into our own immediate 21st century present, into the light of science and technology, as previewed by Heidegger.

We are now especially enfolded in a "techno-geneticism" of potential *replication*. What this means "in essence" is a genetic prolongation of *for the time being* into an end-stopped future.

Technology is a metaphysics at its end

What is at stake? Death is, in essence, a potency without *further necessity*. The meaning of life is therefore without further need of additional sense. Technology has brought us finally to our meaning by putting an end to it. Heidegger wants us to go back and rethink – not where we've gone wrong but where we've been perilously right, "a turn" which might be simplified like this …

Someone might rightly object that, even if the disappearance of death were possible, it would not eliminate absurdity.

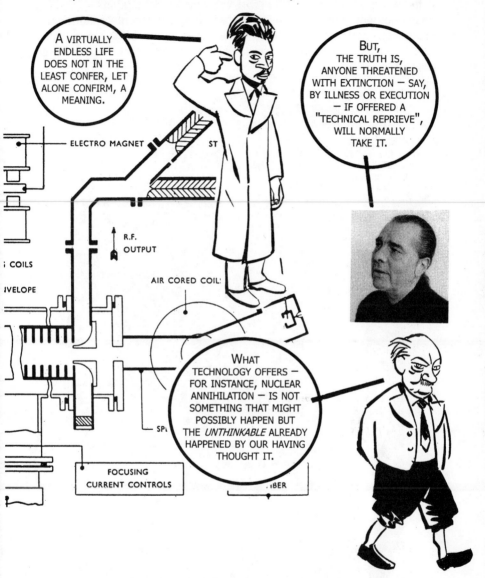

A VIRTUALLY ENDLESS LIFE DOES NOT IN THE LEAST CONFER, LET ALONE CONFIRM, A MEANING.

BUT, THE TRUTH IS, ANYONE THREATENED WITH EXTINCTION — SAY, BY ILLNESS OR EXECUTION — IF OFFERED A "TECHNICAL REPRIEVE", WILL NORMALLY TAKE IT.

ELECTRO MAGNET   ST

R.F. OUTPUT

COILS

VELOPE

AIR CORED COIL

WHAT TECHNOLOGY OFFERS — FOR INSTANCE, NUCLEAR ANNIHILATION — IS NOT SOMETHING THAT MIGHT POSSIBLY HAPPEN BUT THE *UNTHINKABLE* ALREADY HAPPENED BY OUR HAVING THOUGHT IT.

SP

FOCUSING CURRENT CONTROLS

BER

Heidegger's point is that what we normally take on offer from technology (its technical "remedies") does not require *all of the event* in store, for instance, *actual* nuclear holocaust or *actual* elimination of death. In his terms, we are already left over to the "boundless etcetera" of technological permanence.

The anti-geneticist Kirilov

In the aftermath of technicized reprieve, meaning is therefore postponement, deferral – the always "about-to-be" of some betterment in a condition of entropic sameness. I imagine the engineer Kirilov alive today (maybe as a dissident geneticist) who once died for "no God" and now for "no death" …

There is in all of us a sense of "blasphemy" in the idea of an untermed, indefinitely prolonged life, despite our natural aversion to, and evasion of, death.

The limit-situation of meaning

What is it to live *without limit*? From the Latin, *limen* (threshold), *limitis* (border). It is to exist inauthentically in Heidegger's designation. Being can only disclose itself at all in the "primordial limit-situation of Being-towards-death".

DASEIN IS THROWN BY ANXIETY INTO THE INDEFINITENESS OF ITS LIMIT-SITUATION, AND THEREBY GAINS ITS POTENTIALITY FOR BEING A WHOLE.

HEIDEGGER SPEAKS OF "MAN" AS *DASEIN*, LITERALLY IN GERMAN, *BEING-THERE*, WHICH PRESUMES AN *ASTONISHMENT* AT BEING AT ALL, EASILY LOST IN EVERYDAY FAMILIARITY OF "JUST BEING".

What Heidegger aims at, in simplest terms, is that being "in limit" (consider, carefully what that says) cannot be otherwise than *futural*, and this means "bringing death into one's present". Meaning is therefore the limit of the possible, unveiled for me by my anticipation of the "nothing" I am faced with.

What Existentialism isn't

Meaning is given to me by my nothingness? What can that mean? I have not even yet defined Existentialism and am already involved in its "austere technicalities". One thing is made clear. I will not find any *pre-established meaning* in reply to the question of suicide, either in Heidegger, Sartre or Camus. "Go to the Christian Existentialists", someone will advise. Perhaps later; but for now I am as well off with Beckett's metaphysical quip …

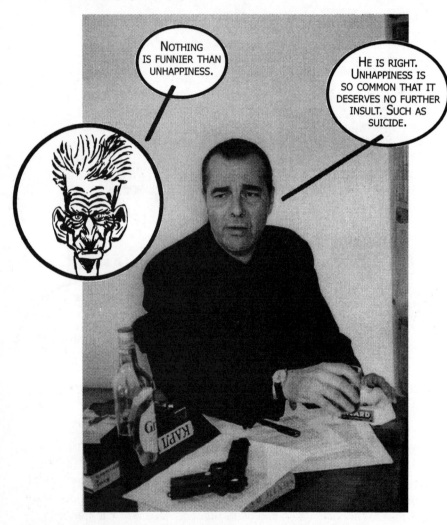

I will meet with further discouragements to establishing what Existentialism is. A better course may be for me to discover what it *isn't*.

I have already agreed not to be misled by colourful terms like "anguish". I have also agreed to disavow literature, to persist in the study of this "austere teaching", such as I will get from Heidegger's lecture-room extremism. I even begin to see a glimmer of sense in disclaiming pre-established meaning as itself an evasion. Existentialism is perhaps at bottom nothing but a study of subsidiary "evasions into meaning". Camus himself, the only one who writes with steadfastly non-technical Mozartian clarity, says exactly the same …

THE TYPICAL ACT OF ELUDING, THE FATAL EVASION … IS HOPE. HOPE OF ANOTHER LIFE ONE MUST "DESERVE" OR TRICKERY OF THOSE WHO LIVE NOT FOR LIFE ITSELF BUT FOR SOME GREAT IDEA THAT WILL TRANSCEND IT, REFINE IT, GIVE IT A MEANING, AND BETRAY IT.

WELL, AT LEAST THIS IS ONE AGREEMENT. WHAT OTHER DISCOURAGEMENTS CAN I POSSIBLY STILL FACE?

Is no one an Existentialist?

There is indeed one more discouragement that amounts to an impasse. No one agrees to being classified an Existentialist.

I CALL THE EXISTENTIAL ATTITUDE *PHILOSOPHICAL SUICIDE*. HOW ELSE TO START FROM THE WORLD'S LACK OF MEANING AND END UP BY FINDING A MEANING AND A DEPTH TO IT.

CAMUS DISQUALIFIES HIMSELF FROM EXISTENTIALISM BY REMAINING RESOLUTELY AN *ABSURDIST*.

THINKING LETS BEING BE – THAT MUST BE UNDERSTOOD AS MY IRREVOCABLE DISTANCE FROM EXISTENTIALISM.

THE ONLY PHILOSOPHY TODAY IS MARXISM. UNTIL NOW, EXISTENTIALISM HAS BEEN A PARASITICAL IDEOLOGY ON ITS MARGIN.

Convalescence of memory

Disavowals, disqualifications and continuous deferrals – where will this end? I spoke of an obscure "betrayal" at the heart of Existentialism. "Denial" might be truer to its nature. The question is – denial of what?

Existentialism originates by *infidelity* to Edmund Husserl's phenomenology. I seek convalescence of memory in that story. It is told principally of two rivals in the claim for Existentialism – Heidegger and Sartre – who both disclaim it, and its founder by default or misapprehension, Husserl. And that is how it should be in a thirty-year war waged in confusion against a "science" of phenomenology.

The origin of Existentialism

My scenario is reduced to a trio of antagonists. I journey back to a time before Existentialism when its origin is a question of *where* these three are placed. I begin with Sartre in 1933 whose route does lead to a "discovery" of Existentialism. He spent that year in Berlin studying Husserl in depth and Heidegger to some extent. He discovered in them an "area history" of "oppositions, agreements, misunderstandings, distortions, denials, surpassings …".

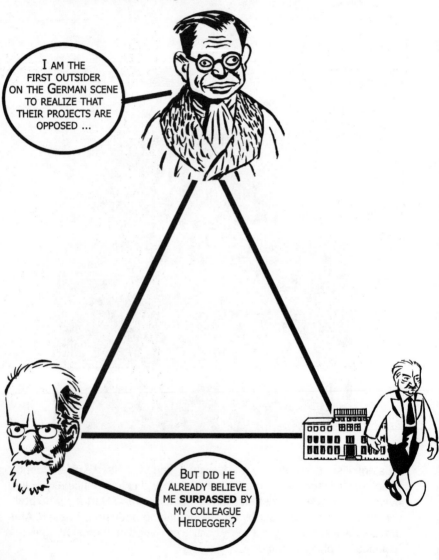

And where is Heidegger?

Heidegger had been Husserl's assistant at Freiburg University from 1919 to 1923. As intimate co-worker, he benefited from "the freest possible access to Husserl's private papers". He succeeded to Husserl's Chair of Philosophy at Freiburg in 1928 and in April 1933 was made Rector of that university. Heidegger's inaugural Rectorship address came out in notorious support for Hitler's recently elected government.

A victim of *Gleichschaltung*

1933 was the crux year of institutional ***Gleichschaltung***, which meant "bringing into step" with Nazi doctrine, in effect, the state control of all public life from which non-Aryans were legally banned. We know the dread sequel to that …

But could the **end** have been foreseen in 1933?

How did the *Gleichschaltung* affect Husserl? It outlawed him as a Jew from public platforms in Germany, his teaching licence was withdrawn, he became a "non-person" by racial decree. He was at least free to lecture in Prague in 1935 on *The Crisis of European Sciences and Transcendental Phenomenology*. I am left to imagine how that lecture too, like Viktor Frankl's, was almost precluded by a descent of "Night and Fog".

A philosophy relevant to life

The "crisis" identified by Husserl is indeed an "existential" one, but in his terms, of a science *philosophically relevant* to life. As such, it predates Nazism and will persist as the single most decisive issue of the 20th century. Heidegger's professed Nazism obscures the significance of his earlier desertion from Husserl's phenomenology. **Karl Jaspers** (1883-1969), who had applied phenomenology to psychiatry in 1911, ventured first into *Existenzphilosophie* but without Heidegger's political lapse.

HUSSERL'S CALL FOR A "RIGOROUS SCIENCE" OF PHENOMENOLOGY IN 1913 TURNED ME AGAINST IT …

… BECAUSE HE'D DISCOVERED KIERKEGAARD BY THEN, WHICH CLINCHED AN "EXISTENTIALISM".

EVEN I, NO FRIEND OF JASPERS' **EXISTENZPHILOSOPHIE**, ADMIRED HIS UNFLINCHING ANTI-NAZISM.

The spectre of phenomenology

What would I in the 1930s have made of this "area history" dense with "oppositions"? Sartre is blamed for misapprehending Husserl as the father of Existentialism. But it is unhelpful to insist correctly that phenomenology is a science of "transcendental subjectivity". We're left imagining some kind of New Age "Tao of physics". Better to think of Husserl as the ghost of Hamlet's father, the betrayed and slain king, who sets the drama in action. Or is he the "false memory syndrome" of Hamlet's bad conscience?

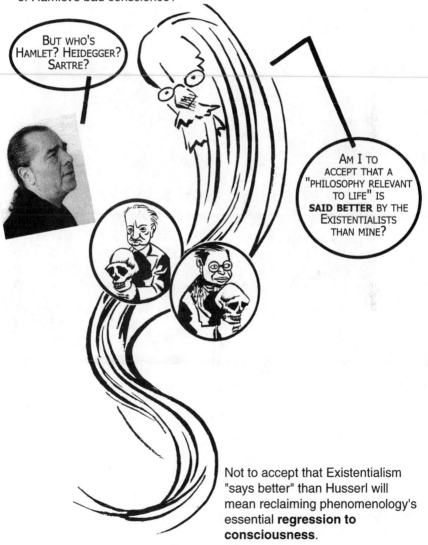

BUT WHO'S HAMLET? HEIDEGGER? SARTRE?

AM I TO ACCEPT THAT A "PHILOSOPHY RELEVANT TO LIFE" IS **SAID BETTER** BY THE EXISTENTIALISTS THAN MINE?

Not to accept that Existentialism "says better" than Husserl will mean reclaiming phenomenology's essential **regression to consciousness**.

The looking-glass rivals

"Regression to consciousness"? What's that? Have I fallen upside-down into psychoanalysis? I note some odd resemblances. In the same year, 1900, Husserl publishes *Logical Investigations*; **Sigmund Freud** (1856-1939) his *Interpretation of Dreams* – two irreconcilable sciences of consciousness and the unconscious – yet also both are similarly Jews, born in Moravia and of near equal life-span. They even look alike …

Jung broke with Freud in 1913; but his likeness to Heidegger comes in 1934 when he accepted the presidency of the Nazi-sponsored German Association for Psychotherapy.

So much for the approximations. The difference is that Husserl's "regression to consciousness" stands glaringly at odds with Freud's meaning of regression and its accepted concomitant, the unconscious.

In what sense does consciousness exist, *absolutely*, not as a naturally pre-given "existence" that psychoanalysis presupposes, not as an illusion, not as an epiphenomenon of the brain that cognitive science argues? What unprecedented "science" excludes all these positions from its research?

Husserl's manifesto of a vocation

How far in non-conformity Husserl stands from all normally accepted empirical presuppositions is best said in his own words, a credo of his vocation to phenomenology.

*From the defects of science ... there proceeds the philosophical demand for a presuppositionless beginning, for a new life of knowledge, a truly radical life; the demand for a life inaugurating a science founded on an absolute justification. ... But this absolute radicalism, for him who wishes to become a philosopher in this most authentic sense of the word, implies his submitting to a corresponding decision which will engage his life in an absolutely radical manner, a decision which will make of his life an **absolutely devoted life**. This is a decision through which the subject becomes self-determining, and even rigorously so – to the very depths of his personality – committed to what is best in itself in the universal realm of intellectual values and committed, for his entire life-time, to the idea of the supreme Good ... the subject chooses [supreme knowledge] as his veritable 'vocation', for which he decides and is decided once for all, to which he is absolutely devoted **as a practical ego.***

from *Cartesian Meditations* (1929-31)

Husserl's exacting science is easier to betray than to follow – and he wanted no followers but a "gnostic community" of co-workers to carry on the infinitely unfinishable job of philosophy. We might understand Existentialism from the start – with Jaspers' earliest departure to it – as an impatience with science. So why does Husserl's manifesto begin with the "defects" of science? He is clear in his 1935 Prague lecture. Planck's quantum "indeterminacy" or Einstein's so-called "relativity" might undermine Newton's classical physics, but physics itself remains an exact science.

It is not the exactness of exact science that troubles Husserl, but the matter-of-fact *grantedness* of its objectivity.

The subject-object differential

You would think that "exactness" and "objectivity" are the same. As a criterion, maybe, but for Husserl it leaves gaping the simple yet irksome problem of the subject-object differential. Consider two words in this sentence: "Things do not **exist** by virtue of their **explanation**." Or do they? What is this **exist** if not an unawares **explanation**? Let's try a sentence even more germane to phenomenology ...

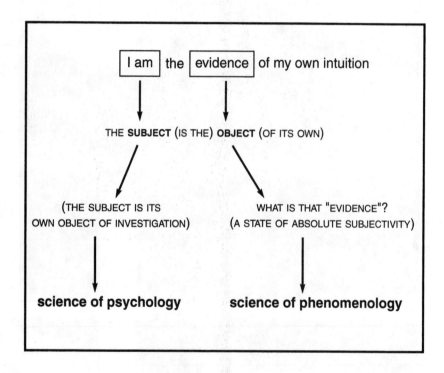

I am the evidence of my own intuition

THE **SUBJECT** (IS THE) **OBJECT** (OF ITS OWN)

(THE SUBJECT IS ITS OWN OBJECT OF INVESTIGATION)

WHAT IS THAT "EVIDENCE"? (A STATE OF ABSOLUTE SUBJECTIVITY)

science of psychology

science of phenomenology

It is symptomatic of a malaise to say that science and a "philosophy relevant to life" are tragically drifting apart. That's vague. What does it mean under analysis? What "drifts apart" is already intrinsic to the subject who splits into **existential** and **theoretical** being. Existential means being *my own presence* in this world. Theoretical means being the subject of *some other* impersonal evidence.

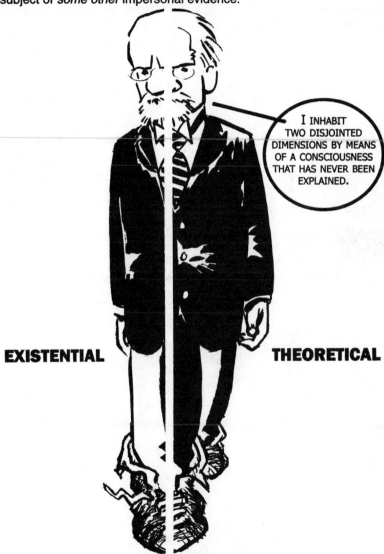

A guiding thread through the forthcoming maze …
reductionism would not be possible were it not for the irreducible complexity of mind.

Natural and theoretical attitudes

This world in all its manifest pre-givenness is the one in which I too am given as existential subject. "Here I am" says it all in transparent obviousness. "That's how things are, no question of it." But this unproblematic *natural attitude* shares the same object world from which a *theoretical attitude* of science outcrops. For, of course, science does question how "things are as they are". We normally overlook that decisive psychological switch from one attitude to another.

WE SWITCH **CONVICTIONS** – FROM A TRANSPARENT VIEW OF "HOW THINGS ARE" TO AN **INFERENCE** FROM THEM THAT GAINS ITS ENTIRE HOLD ON OUR CERTITUDE.

So it is that science – a theoretical certainty – comes entirely to occupy the field of our natural attitude and is thereby "naturalized" as the only world view.

The unquestionable pre-givenness of a world is one in which I am both *explained* by and *explainer* of the laws which govern its discovery. Have I forgotten something in this tidy process of answering to the world in which I undoubtedly am? Yes, I forget *how* I am in it. Not in any religious sense, but simply how *appearance* is given to the world.

PRECISELY THAT IS MY QUESTION — "IN WHAT SENSE **IS** CONSCIOUSNESS?"

The natural attitude is normally *what is* taken for granted. By stressing "what is", I awaken my uncertainty of its grantedness. I see for once how the world is *already placed* for me in it.

A case-history of scepticism

Husserl says that he owes his question to that most ruthless of enlightened sceptics, **David Hume** (1711-76), for whom all our most cherished natural beliefs, including *identity* itself, reduce to a psychological fiction.

HOW IS THE NAÏVE OBVIOUSNESS OF OUR CERTAINTY OF THIS WORLD IN WHICH WE LIVE TO BE MADE **ITSELF** UNDERSTANDABLE?

NO ONE HAS EVER FULLY REPLIED TO HUME'S SUBTLE PROBLEM.

NOT SO! I BEGAN WITH THE ONLY POSSIBLE ANSWER TO SUCH EVIDENCE ...

Ego cogito, ergo sum

René Descartes (1596-1650) and Husserl are in curious symmetry. Both originate in a mathematics cognizant of the pioneering physics of their day – **Galileo**'s (1564-1642) for Descartes, quantum theory for Husserl. Both are concerned with a naïve question of *what is certainty* that sheds all previous philosophy. Descartes begins with his: "How do I know for sure that anything science proposes is objectively true?" In answer to that, he takes the unprecedented step of doubting the validity of all accepted convictions.

Descartes' great error

Descartes performed the severest reduction of the world to yield one indubitable fact. Only the "I" which *thinks the reduction* is absolutely certain. *Ego cogitans* (the "thinking I") is a self-deductive axiom that saves a residue evidence of the world from which all the rest can be inferred. Descartes felt authorized to pursue objectivity on the grounds of **secured subjectivity**.

BUT IS THIS **EGO** AN EXISTENTIAL OR THEORETICAL SUBJECT?

DESCARTES' GREATEST DISCOVERY IS HIS GREATEST ERROR ...

WHY DO YOU SAY THAT?

The world undoubtedly is; but my ego which thinks it is not some *thing* in that world. Where in the world of existing things will you find "I think"? Consciousness of something is *psychical inexistence*.

Res cogitans: the thinking thing

Mind for Descartes is a unique thing apprehensible only to introspection. A loophole opens wide to scepticism. Either this mind "thing" is an exorcisable "ghost in the machine" or it must be a legitimate subject-matter of objective science, in its case, empirical psychology. We proceed to the latter position with **John Locke** (1632-1704).

WHAT IS MIND? A "BLANK SHEET" ON WHICH A **SENSE-DATA CONTINUUM** IS INSCRIBED.

HE REPLACES MY "I" CERTAINTY WITH A MERE IMPRESSIONABLE BLANK ...

AND WHY NOT TAKE THAT NEXT STEP OF REDUCING "I" TO **RES COGITANS**, A THINKING **SUBSTANCE**?

The sceptical booby-trap

A thinking substance reduced to its material constituents of sense data has at least the merit of appearing certain. But is it? Might not the undeniable permanency of sense data in mind further imply that *sensations alone exist*? What certain proof does it give that the world *actually is*? Locke's view is reversed by the imp of perversity, **George Berkeley** (1685-1753), Bishop of Cloyne.

WHAT IF I SHOULD REGARD THE PHYSICAL WORLD AS A FIGMENT OF MY OWN MENTAL IMPRESSIONS? **ESSE EST PERCIPI**: TO BE IS TO BE PERCEIVED. THERE IS NO WORLD "OUTSIDE" THIS IDEA I HAVE OF PERCEIVING IT.

WHY STOP WITH A FICTITIOUS WORLD "OUT THERE"? IS NOT THE MIND TOO A FICTION OF ITS OWN PERCEPTION?

We've traced a vicious circle from Descartes' ego certainty to Hume's fiction of identity.

The existential sacrifice

No matter how far radical scepticism goes, it remains in the natural attitude and its perplexing world of pre-givenness. Is there no escape from its circle? There is – through science, which apparently "transcends" Hume's question of "naïve obviousness". This is the paradox that Husserl insists we grasp.

SCIENCE IS ALWAYS THEORETICALLY POSSIBLE ON THE BASIS OF AN EXISTENTIAL SACRIFICE ...

... A **FORGETFULNESS** OF BEING, I PREFER TO NAME IT.

Heidegger's proviso suggests to me that Existentialism is met with here – in the crisis of science – where I am not normally expected to find it.

Whose "crisis" is it?

Heidegger rightly means that the "crisis" of science is not its own but ours by unmindfulness of how science came entirely to occupy our horizon of *being in the world*. An impatient view of Husserl's position. For him, science is by now so divorced from philosophy that we cannot see them originally wedded. Indeed, philosophy has succumbed to the commonsense nihilism of no connection at all to real "foolproof" science.

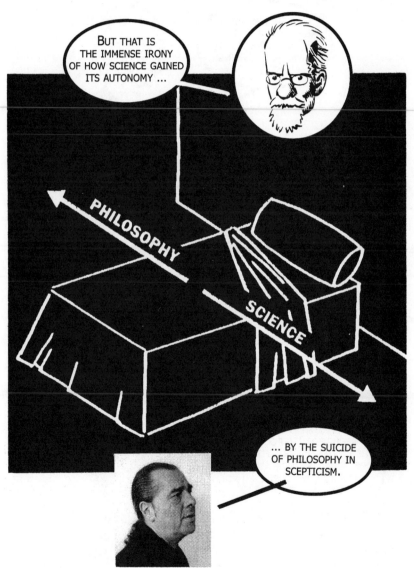

Suicide by economy of thought

Scepticism liquidates philosophy by a series of reductions from Descartes onwards which increasingly "economizes" on the thought of "what is". Until we are finally left marooned with scientific **reductionism** which is the essentialist thesis of *nothing but*, such as: "red is nothing but light of a certain wave length".

The "defect" of science is its "defection" from the pre-givenness of the world to a post-mortem one of theorized objectivities. It does not thereby become any less "exact", on the contrary – but that was never Husserl's worry. His own undefected science is said in the maxim, "Back to the things themselves", by which he means a regression to the originally pre-given data of consciousness itself.

Husserl's "idealism" will be Existentialism's excuse for deserting his science.

Cartesian meditations on *epochē*

Husserl begins all over again where Descartes began, yes, in *reduction*. Not by accident he goes back to the original Greek word for it, *epochē*, coined by the founder himself of scepticism, **Pyrrho of Elis** (c. 360-272 BC). It means both "to intend" and "cease from" – an immovable standpoint – recommended as a suspension of all philosophy.

Heidegger's devotion to early Greek "pre-Socratic" philosophy will not permit any hint that it might have originated in scepticism.

Heidegger's famous question, "What is 'is'?", restates the primordial Truth of Being, "that **What Is**, is", first spoken by **Parmenides of Elea** (c. 515-445 BC). In reply, Husserl would signal another pre-Socratic teacher, **Protagoras** (c. 485-415 BC), who says that "Man is the measure of all things". This is no arrogant claim to knowledge, but a statement of *reductive limit*. A theoretical attitude – which the Greeks are first to adopt on the world of being – at once recognizes itself as less than is natural to the richness of "what is".

KNOWLEDGE ALREADY SPLITS INTO TWO GOALS ...

THEORETICAL INTEREST (SCIENCE)

EXISTENTIAL SELF-INTEREST (WISDOM)

The Husserlian *epochē*

Epochē is for Husserl the unfulfilled promise of scepticism. What does all scepticism want? Certitude, even at the cost of its own suicidal reduction. What is lost in this momentous progress to scientific exactitude (for which *existential* certitude is sacrificed)? The existence of consciousness is omitted. Heidegger will instead say that the "history of Being" is forgotten, not consciousness, of no interest to him.

OUR POSITIONS ARE CLOSE YET SO DIFFERENT BECAUSE OF THE STATUS WE GIVE TO "EXISTENTIAL" IN OUR INVESTIGATIONS.

"EXISTENTIAL" IS NOT A WORD OFTEN FOUND IN HUSSERL.

MY AIM IS CARTESIAN IN GIVING CERTAINTY TO CONSCIOUSNESS THAT HE LEFT HOSTAGE TO SCEPTICISM.

In what sense "is" consciousness?

The certain existence of consciousness must begin for Husserl with the fact that it is *no thing*. An unpromising start, apparently. How can what isn't, be? And worse, be *certain*? The question is at obvious antipode to Heidegger's.

It would be better to say consciousness "stands out" in the presence of the world, for the case is that I am a presence to my *self*-perception because *everything else* is a presence for me. *Appearance* itself is somehow a manifestation of this non-thingness of consciousness.

A parenthetical gaze

How can I *regress* to the origin of what is "appearing" for me? My thoughts are habitually in continuous flow. I see something that "gets" my attention – a tree, let's say. *Epochē* – I "cease", I interrupt myself and turn my attention back from the object manifested to the manifesting act of consciousness. I stabilize its evanescence.

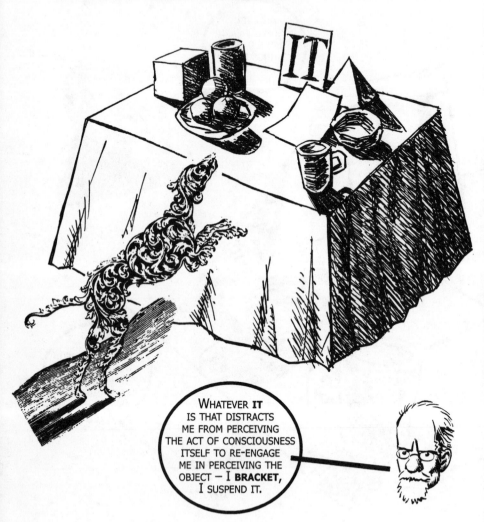

WHATEVER **IT** IS THAT DISTRACTS ME FROM PERCEIVING THE ACT OF CONSCIOUSNESS ITSELF TO RE-ENGAGE ME IN PERCEIVING THE OBJECT – I **BRACKET**, I SUSPEND IT.

What is *there* forgoes its perceptual efficacy but is in no sense presumed inexistent. On the contrary. Its existence threatens to engulf my *epoché* in failure. I attempt to neutralize the validity of things in order to seize consciousness manifesting itself.

THIS IS NO GAME, BUT A PERILOUS IMMERSION THAT I ACKNOWLEDGE IS "CONTRARY TO NATURE".

EPOCHĒ'S INVALIDATION OF THE WORLD'S PRE-GIVENNESS IS VERY LIKE THE "METAPHYSICAL SUICIDE" I SPOKE OF EARLIER.

The result of practised *epoché* is a vertigo that succeeds in the *falling away* of the world. I gaze into an abyss as I do in contemplating suicide.

A template of suicide

Do I overcharge *epochē* with a likeness to suicide? The sceptics' reduction of identity in the end to fiction is as near as I can come to actual suicide, to a "template" of it. Husserl's *epochē* is unlike that. Or is it? Does he not affirm the *psychical inexistence* of the ego reduced to its consciousness? I go back to Camus' question of suicide and rephrase it …

WHAT IS PECULIAR TO HUMAN EXISTENCE THAT IT CAN BEGIN WITH A QUESTION OF ITS OWN ENDING? WHAT IS THIS "IT"?

The question ceases to be existential to become phenomenological when I realize "not *who* but *what is it* I dispose of?" To "dispose of" is a pregnant ambiguity. It serves usefully to manifest what suicide hides – not simply "the person" on whom is performed (self-)homicide – but the subject presupposed for invalidation. Put more strongly: this pre-given subject that "I" kill does not exist.

Husserl was aware of a suicide template in *epochē*'s disposal of "I myself". An incident helps to illustrate this. Husserl invited Heidegger to assist him in writing an article on phenomenology for the 1927 *Encyclopaedia Britannica*. Husserl wrote the following in his draft copy …

Heidegger's dissatisfaction with "epochist" consciousness finds its replacement in *Being and Time* with the mysterious catchword *Dasein*, which not only says "being there" but also designates "the entity, *man himself*".

A technicolour Joseph's-coat of suicide

The incident is complicated by a note on suicide from Husserl's manuscripts of the 1920s. Heidegger admits his "freest possible access" to such papers. What does he find in this one?

*… need I, need any person be? Does there lie in the evidence of the "I am" more than the evidence of the person in relation to a presumptive world, and why should there not be able to be a "multi-coloured" self? Is the opposite not in fact thinkable; can I not, as it were, commit **personal** suicide by way of dismantling the associative constitution of experience, while my life, even if it is objectively significationless, nonetheless remains as the foundation for this suicidal possibility …*

A "MULTI-COLOURED SELF"? WHAT DOES HE MEAN BY DIVESTING THIS JOSEPH'S-COAT SELF IN "PERSONAL" SUICIDE?

A sceptic skeleton in the closet

"… need I, need any person be?" is a question so to speak *technicized* by Heidegger in a 1929 lecture, "What is Metaphysics?", in which he famously asks: "Why are there things rather than nothing?", taken as he says from the metaphysician **G.W. Leibniz** (1646-1716).

A REPLY TO HUSSERL? HIDDEN AWAY LIKE A NAGGING SORE TOOTH IN **BEING AND TIME** IS THIS …

"A sceptic can no more be refuted than the Being of truth can be 'proved'. And if any sceptic of the kind who denies the truth, factically **is**, *he does* **not** *even* **need** *to be refuted. In so far as he* **is**, *and has understood himself in this Being, he has obliterated* Dasein *in the desperation of suicide; and in doing so, he has also obliterated truth. Because* Dasein, *for its own part, cannot first be subjected to proof, the necessity of truth cannot be proved either."*

Sartre on suicide

Sartre in *Being and Nothingness* totally humanizes the inhuman elements of Husserlian consciousness and Heideggerian being. Existence is for him literally *freedom* that the "nothingness" of consciousness bestows on me to make of life a project of my choice. Meaning is what the future alone can give to life. To die is to receive no further meaning.

An answer plainly, lucidly humanist; right but again impatient. It does not reply to what is *unintelligible* in freedom.

"In-itself" and "for-itself"

What is freedom grounded on? Sartre replies: on the *nothingness* of consciousness which effects a "psychic gap" – and imaginative distance – between myself and the world of non-conscious reality. Out there is only an undifferentiated plenitude of Being-*in*-itself whose material resistance to me gains form and significance by my activity of consciousness. The person is solely this act of Being-*for*-itself, hence its terrifying freedom.

FREEDOM IS OUR INESCAPABLE CONDITION WHICH – TRY AS WE CAN TO EVADE IT BY FLIGHT INTO SELF-DECEPTION – IS A **CHOICE** TOO.

I TAKE THE POOR MAN'S VIEW OF FREEDOM – SOMETHING ELSE I CAN'T AFFORD TO WASTE.

Sartre's name for his monumental opus invites comparison with Heidegger's *Being and Time*; its subtitle, "Outline of a Phenomenological Ontology", seems to enlist Husserl. How close or not is he to either?

Being free for death ...

Sartre privileges the free act of mind as somehow *constituting* being, a humanist gloss that misconstrues Heidegger's assertion: "only as long as there is human being is there (*es gibt*) such a thing as Being". Which does of course sound "existential": Being is accessible only for *human* being. Heidegger's *Letter on Humanism*, 1949 – that is, after the war, and against Sartre's Existentialist humanism – qualifies the true sense of *es gibt*, "it gives".

In other words, Being isn't merely what "occurs" to us, but is a gift whose giving can be withdrawn. Human being is in no way "constitutive" of Being.

... a resoluteness for history

What is freedom for Heidegger? And what is it *before the war*? In *Being and Time*, 1927, he says "the outright goal of *Dasein* is Being-free for death", a resoluteness in face of which only **authentic historicizing** is possible. I cannot read these pages without a chill of foretelling doom – and remarking on Heidegger's no change of mind *after* the event in 1949 ...

"*If* Dasein, *by anticipation, lets death become powerful in itself, then, as free for death,* Dasein *understands itself in its own **superior power**, the power of its finite freedom, so that in this freedom, which "is" only in its having chosen to make such a choice, it can take over the **powerlessness** of abandonment to its having done so, and can thus come to have a clear vision for the accidents of the Situation that has been disclosed.*"

... also in 1927

There is opportunist Will to Power in Heidegger, perhaps too in Sartre but for the opposed reason of Resistance. Heidegger's idea of freedom is an unpeopled "letting Being be". Is this a question of letting the world take its own course; or a disguised "decisionism" that abandons us to a *superior cause*?

I STRAY INTO THE BIG "ISSUE" OF HISTORY IN WHICH HUSSERL IS SAID TO BE DISINTERESTED.

RECALL WHAT I ALSO SAID IN **1927** ...

"... *life is a living-onward that has life behind it as well as beside it, but not in a merely natural externality, much rather in the inwardness of an* **intentional tradition**. *We may also say that life is through and through historical; living-onward is a going forth out of a life from which it has its prefiguration of sense and Being, a prefiguration that, as historical, encloses its own historical lineage as something that can again be disclosed, which can be unveiled, which can be drawn out of it by questioning.*" (**Lectures on "Nature and Spirit", 1927**)

Does philosophy have office hours?

Heidegger "exalts death", says the Marxist philosopher **T.W. Adorno** (1903-69), and transforms it into a "professional secret for academics". A devastating sarcasm; but then, Adorno was himself an academic, so too Husserl, and even Sartre, product of the élite Ecole Normale, took his mandarin "chair" to the Café de Flore. A philosopher's comedy? For Husserl, in 1935, it is a grave question of *vocation*. Rightly, he notes, do the existentials mock the bourgeois time-keeping of "professional" thinkers.

DO I PERFORM **EPOCHĒ** WITHIN OFFICE HOURS, THEN GO HOME AND ... RELAX?

NOTHING WRONG WITH THAT, IS THERE?

Living in (im)partiality

We all expect to relax from our everyday occupations. How far to take this? To those in advanced genetic research? Or the commandant of a death camp who sweats his hard day and then expects – what? Is that grotesquely exaggerated? I, we, all of us live in a dichotomy of normality, a duplex living-*versus*-living, i.e., in conflict between living *for* and living *on* something.

WE SAY "HE LIVES FOR HIS WORK". IT IS HIS GOAL OR END IN ITSELF.

OTHERS LIVE MORE SENSIBLY **ON** THEIR WORK. IT PROVIDES FOR CONSUMPTION AND LEISURE.

Either way, we live in a sort of **impartiality**, but always partially "within hours", that both equally permit of suspension of self-awareness, either by evasion or simulated ignorance. What is a "philosophic life", then?

The life problem of vocation

Husserl reflected intensely on that life problem of vocation in philosophy. What is vocation? It used to mean a call to the priesthood, a "profession" of faith. For the philosopher, it is a call to heedfulness but unprofessed unless he calls *others* to heedfulness. Heidegger and Sartre make of this "call to others" a summons to be …

… **AUTHENTIC** LIVING TOWARDS BEING IN HISTORY.

… **COMMITMENT** TO BEING UNDECEIVED.

THIS IS STILL EXISTENTIAL AND STILL ONLY A "PART" CORRELATIVE TO THE THEORETICAL.

Impartiality of mind depends on being partial. "Partial" is the entire cargo bearing on the existential and theoretical split subject. How do I understand this?

Entireness in parenthesis

It would seem insurmountable to get "behind" what is there for me in a given world of which I am entirely part. Husserl's act of *epochē* intends to "lift the veil" of this undeniably *true* condition of being. Crucially, then, it is not the truth but the *condition of givenness* – both the objective world in its entirety and my "I" being naturally in it – that *epochē* suspends in order to regress to *what is consciousness* as itself the absolute first beginning of any possible *appearance*.

"BEING GIVEN" IS PUT IN PARENTHESIS …

IT IS NOT THE "BEING" OF THINGS **EPOCHĒ** SUSPENDS BUT BEING'S **CLAIM** ON CONSCIOUSNESS.

Husserl's *epochē* suspends (brackets) the "I's" psychological presupposition of givenness. Things remain truthfully in place but are now **unintelligible**.

To see originally

Unintelligible? Yes, as in the question earlier posed to Sartre's notion of freedom. Is it unveiled by "grounding" it in nothingness? Hardly. So too, Husserl can be reprimanded: is your "absolute first beginning" feasible? What "other" beginning can there be to a plainly obvious world and my idea of it? It is obvious, in my natural attitude, but by no means self-evident that what presents itself to me is the *secured origin* of my knowledge. Scepticism plays havoc with that.

HOW CAN I SEE THINGS **ORIGINALLY** WITHOUT READING INTO THEM ANY OF OUR THEORETICAL HYPOTHESES AND SOLUTIONS?

The journey is one of regression to a "presuppositionless" state – if that's thinkable.

The problem of intentionality

"What is" is unceasing: from this, *epochē* wants to "cease". Difficult, if not impossible, because consciousness is always *of* something. Such is the appeal of things that even I myself am something *of* my awareness. Of course, it is obvious if not trivial to realize that thinking is intentionally *directed on* something. Husserl does not hurry from this naïve, trivial fact of intentionality which for him has two aspects …

It is by insight into this second *constitutive* aspect that reality becomes unintelligible.

Cutting the umbilical cord

When I become suddenly aware in astonishment that the world in its entirety *is* and can only make such *appearance* in consciousness, I have absolutely no explanation how some supposed "life" of consciousness can accomplish this wonder. How does existence manifest itself as something *meant* for authentication by experience? Reality of being at this moment turns uncanny, incomprehensible.

"I can't get over it" is precisely what reality means for us. To tamper with that natural tie invites "being at sea".

Only a question of words

The questionable aspect of intentionality – that by which I mysteriously "constitute" things in my consciousness – leads me to fall into a "transcendentally naïve" state. Here is a word, *transcendence*, and the equally unfriendly *immanence*, that philosophers frequently use. To mean what, simply? Let's look at their Latin roots …

HEIDEGGER IS RIGHT THAT ROOT ORIGINS OF WORDS OFTEN SAY **WHERE** WE ARE IN THE FORGOTTEN "HISTORY" OF BEING.

trans (beyond) *scendere* (climb) = "go above"

im (in) *manere* (to stay) = "stay put"

Immanence is the ground of presupposed being: it "stays put" as given in the natural attitude.

Transcendence questions the validity of any possible claim to being: it doesn't "stay put" in the given but threatens to "go above" for additional clarification.

There is no beyond language

Or is Heidegger wrong, and "being" is only a question of words? *Il n'y pas de hors-texte*, says **Jacques Derrida** (b. 1930), meaning: outside of language, there is nothing to which we can directly refer, since all language is indicative *only of itself*.

How does language confirm that there is nothing indicative outside itself? It must "go above" its own immanence to have "seen" this. Language (in Derrida's sense of englobing "text") must be *partial* – or how else then recognize what it says "for" anything? Scepticism arrives at its final postmodern camouflage of blaming language as its accessory to doubt.

Abschattungen – perception in profile

The paradox is this: language is partially its own whole. So is everything else we perceive. Our faith in the wholeness of things is not shaken by the fact, crucial to phenomenology, that we actually never see *anything whole*. Things give us their appearance only in *Abschattungen*, in "profiles" that must unfold sequentially. I can see the front of this cup but not *at once* its back. I can see parts of a cube but not *at once* all sides of it. How is this manifold of perspectives re-constituted as "one and the same" object?

Phenomenology requires an immense *slowing down* of the mind's natural tempo of perception, precisely to "see" the essences of things suspended in temporality.

Funes the Memorious

I have a story that can help us. The Argentinian writer **Jorge Luis Borges** (1899-1986) tells it of Funes whose brain injury caused him to endure "implacable memory" – *he cannot forget anything*. Detail is total and vertiginous: "it bothered him that the dog at 3:14 (seen from the side) should have the same name as the dog at 3:15 (seen from the front)." He is unable to reconfigure the whole from its endlessly "memorious" parts.

In fact, what is withdrawn from Funes remembering everything is *time*, and it is for that reason an instructive fiction.

Is undivided attention possible?

I listen to Mozart's Jupiter symphony – better, I try to listen to myself listening. What's happened to the note I've just heard, even as I listen to it?

Music is a *temporal object*. It would be *unhearable* if it did not somehow "exist" in a *stream of consciousness* which can sustain the "now" note, along with the relevant "past" note and the projected "future" note. And my special effort of attention? Must it not choose between *inattention* to the music or to myself? Ordinary language speaks of "stray thoughts", "absent-minded", "lost in thought", that is, of being always *temporally partial*.

Where is invariance?

Existence is, so to speak, "film-like" in its temporality. I am a *living present* that constantly "slips my mind". I live impartially contented in the midst of partial apparitions. Is there nothing *invariant* in this stream of variations? Perhaps only a mathematician – as Husserl was by training in the calculus of variations – would have noticed the peculiar "formal realities" given by intuition …

ONLY INTUITION EVER SEIZES ON "INVARIANT WHOLES" IN THE PURE FORMAL REGIONS OF MATHEMATICS, LOGIC AND GEOMETRY …

These two incongruous figures are resolved as the planes of a pyramid.

Shadows in Plato's cave

Husserl's word *Abschattungen* is literally "adumbrations" in English, and both have the sense of "to represent in shadowy outline". And that brings to mind Plato's story in the *Republic* of prisoners in a cave whose only view of reality is the profiled "shadows of things" cast on the wall by their jailers.

Plato (427-347 BC) accepts only that pure *invariant* "Ideal Forms" are real but unavailable to us in our unenlightened "cave" of everyday perceptions.

Are ideas "real"?

Husserl is accused of a Platonist belief in the *reality of ideas*. Is Plato's idealism akin to Husserl's formalist invariances of intuition? We cannot say that there is "nothing like" the resolved pyramidical planes in reality. But in what sense is such a form "real"? Husserl begins commonsensibly with an object both of us can see …

Husserl's nonconformist Platonism

Husserl's nonconformist Platonism is to hold that all things –
whether *empirical* or *intuitional* – are equally givens. His view can
be stated like this …

> *No evidence can overrule a direct **given** intuition **that I have** of a
> geometrical theorem which in its pure meaning is, and **is** a certain
> **object**, whether we are pleased to call it "ideal" or not.*
>
> *All logic and science would end if the concept "object" did not count
> as an object. Do you see?*

Husserl's so-called "idealism" amounts simply to affirming that intuition's
originally presenting givens cannot be falsely explained away.

What is evidence?

The oddity of Husserl's insight is this. Intuition is final incontrovertible evidence of that which seeks its own incontrovertibility. He uses the stronger Greek word for evidence, *apodicity*, meaning "to show clearly" but also "to receive back in full". In Husserl's own words from *Cartesian Meditations* ...

> An **apodictic** evidence ... is not merely certainty of the affairs or states-of-affairs evident in it; rather it discloses itself to a critical reflection as having the signal peculiarity of being **at the same time the absolute unimaginableness** of their **non-being**, and thus excluding in advance every doubt as "objectless", empty.

BUT THEN, HOW WOULD I EVER KNOW IF I AM NOT IN ERROR?

TIME

SPACE

When the walls sweat

Truth must have a strange aversion to itself. It is always just "about to be" but never quite coincides with itself. I come to a desolate unhappy place of one's own choice, the "state of philosophy", in shabby dilapidation. What I see is the agonizing of thought itself which turns the world grey, arid, until the walls themselves sweat. Life in revenge against me is seeping back in …

I overhear the ironist **Søren Kierkegaard** (1813-55), predecessor of Dostoyevsky's spiteful man from the underground.

Kierkegaard's *dramatis personae*

The Danish philosopher Kierkegaard is not one but a crowd of pseudonymous authors bizarrely named: *Constantine Constantius*, *Johannes de Silentio*, *Victor Eremita*, and so on in plurality. Through them, the lively ambiguities of aesthetics, ethics and metaphysics are voiced as eccentric literature. His credit is to have turned philosophy into a *problem of writing*. Existentialism is totally indebted to him for the colourful categories, anxiety, dread, despair, absurdity, etc., etc., yea, "death" itself included. I listen to a story from Constantine Constantius' book *Repetition* (1843) …

95

Kierkegaard's bogeyman, Hegel

At the very instant the speck chafed Constantine's eye, he "toppled into the abyss of despair" and gave up all hope of "ever feeling myself content *absolutely* ...". That "speck in the eye" alludes to the Gospels, St Matthew 7, 3-5, and the collapsed "world view" is that of **G.W.F Hegel** (1770-1831), the most absolute of system-builders in philosophy.

HOW MUCH DID KIERKEGAARD COMMAND OF HEGEL'S SYSTEM?

ENOUGH TO KNOW HIMSELF IN PERIL FROM THE **AUFHEBUNG**, THE KEYSTONE OF HEGEL'S ENTIRE HISTORICAL SYSTEM OF LOGIC.

Aufhebung requires the English coinage "sublation" to explain that contradictions in history are at once *overcome* but *preserved by elevation* to a higher stage.

Aufhebung seems pretty harmless. Why is Kierkegaard "imperilled"? Sartre answers from his *Search for a Method* (1960) which confesses his way into (and out of) Existentialism. An essential revelation, because, as we now commonly accept, Kierkegaard is the unquestionable founder of Existentialism – and that notion precisely is dismantled by Sartre. He agrees with Kierkegaard on a fundamental *existential* level …

HEGELIANISM NEGLECTS THE **UNSURPASSABLE OPAQUENESS** OF THE LIVED EXPERIENCE …

TRUE ENOUGH. HEGEL IS DISQUIETINGLY ABSOLUTE IN HIS OPTIMISM.

… A TRAGIC EXPERIENCE – A SUFFERING UNTO DEATH – IS MERELY ABSORBED AND **SUBLATED** BY THE SYSTEM IN ITS PASSAGE TOWARDS THE GENUINE HISTORICAL ABSOLUTE.

The unrelieved conscience of being

Kierkegaard's merit is to insist on the primacy of the specifically real over thought. The real cannot be reduced to thought. That "speck in one's eye" opposes its existential *coloration of mood* to the supra-individual transcendent system. Subjective life can never be made the object of formally abstract knowledge.

Falling into faith

What is the problem with Kierkegaard's "transcendence"? It is for him a *mystical* going beyond to God. Not however in any traditional religious sense of a leap "up" to God but "down", a free fall into subjective inwardness of infinite depth. That's where Kierkegaard poses man, on the precipice of the absurd, brought to utmost extremity of *no other possibility* but to fall …

The scandal of faith

Kierkegaard's "fallenness" into absurd faith – that quasi-suicidal transcendence – is his desperate weapon against systematized Hegelian history. He is vexed to madness by Hegel's untroubled view of philosophy's priority over "experience".

Kierkegaard gives the name "Christendom" to a society Christian in name only, virtually atheist by institutionalizing "its own reason" for being Christian. Hegel is disastrously right: genuine experience of faith has been bypassed for historical "reasons of state". No rescue of faith is available except by self-elected absurdity.

A man in dark times

Sartre is in no doubt, and unfair, that Kierkegaard "is certainly not a philosopher" and that Hegel is to be preferred. Kierkegaard lures us into the depths of subjectivity only to make us discover there the unhappiness of man without God – and that is a "surreptitious wish to resuscitate the *transcendent*" for which Sartre now condemns Existentialism. Not his own but that of Kierkegaard's German proponent, Karl Jaspers. Jaspers courageously withstood Nazism before and during the war years in Germany.

HANNAH ARENDT

A MAN IN DARK TIMES WHO RISKED EVERYTHING ON AN **EXISTENZPHILOSOPHIE** OF TOTAL COMMUNICATION ...

ONLY THE CONSTANT URGE TOWARDS TOTAL REVELATION REACHES THE PATH OF COMMUNICATION.

HANNAH ARENDT IS JEWISH

A strategy of pessimism

Jasper's former student and Jewish philosopher **Hannah Arendt** (1906-75) pays him the tribute of "inviolability". Sartre agrees with that but savages the Kierkegaardian "falling" into mystical transcendence that plays hide-and-seek in Jaspers' *Existenzphilosophie*.

TRANSCENDENCE COMES TO US INDIRECTLY BY MEDITATION ON THE UNIVERSAL FAILURE GUARANTEED BY OUR OWN IMPERFECTABILITY ...

THUS HE LEADS US TO DISCOVER TRANSCENDENCE. IN A **PRESENTIMENT** OF IT THAT WE LEARN AT COST FROM OUR OWN FAILURES, IN DEFEAT AND PESSIMISM.

MY WIFE IS JEWISH

... and what might pessimism *incline* us to? A "theological optimism that dares not speak its name". Jaspers speaks instead of "communicability" that must risk reaching out in love to everyone – a clandestine Gospel message.

The failure of science

Jaspers is a Catholic who keeps mute on revealed religion. He confides revelation to pessimism whose task is to eke out a possible transcendence that will always elude us. Jaspers *historicizes* Kierkegaard's "absurd" of transcendent faith to obscure the *real* historic failure – a failure perfectly suited, in Sartre's estimation, to a partially de-Christianized bourgeoisie nostalgic for its past faith. And why suited?

WHY? BECAUSE IT HAS LOST CONFIDENCE IN ITS OWN SCIENTIFIC RATIONALISM.

... THE CORRECTEDNESS OF SCIENCE EQUATES US ALL "IN THEORY" AS **REPLACEABLE POINTS,** NOT AS HUMAN BEINGS. IT FAILS US IN THE ESSENTIALS, THE ETERNAL PROBLEMS ...

DID I NOT GIVE WARNING OF THIS IN 1935?

MY WIFE IS JEWISH

The spectre of Marx

Sartre's issue with Jaspers is not the Husserlian question of science but, more pointedly, *history*. There is admissable validity in Kierkegaard's defence of the existential subject against the juggernaut of Hegel's Absoluteness. History in Hegel's purely idealist surview is *philosophy* in action but only *realized* – a double-edged word – in contemplation.

ISN'T IT NECESSARY, EVEN IN KIERKEGAARD'S **INDIVIDUAL** TERMS, TO SURPASS CONTEMPLATION IN ACTUAL REALIZED ACTION? SO DID MARX INTEND BY AN "END" TO PHILOSOPHY.

SO, THEN, FOR YOU JASPERS COMMITS THE GRAVER CRIME OF REFUSAL TO COOPERATE IN HISTORY ...

... A HISTORY WHICH MARXISTS ARE MAKING. HE WITHDRAWS FROM KIERKEGAARD'S **REALITY OF THE LIVED** TO ARISTOCRATIC INWARDNESS.

A refuge in ivory-tower pessimism therefore suits well a doomed European bourgeoisie unwilling to see its future. Sartre by 1960 is clearly distancing himself from Existentialism altogether to align himself with Marxism at a time of Cold War gridlock in world affairs and a specifically hot one raging in Algeria as it struggles for independence from French colonial rule (1954-62).

Sartre's partner, novelist and philosopher **Simone de Beauvoir** (1908-86), participated with him in launching that journal in 1945.

An Existentialist anti-colonialism

Do I mistake a certain inadvertence in Sartre's veer to Marxism? He seems to overlook what now assimilates him to Kierkegaard. If indeed Kierkegaard may be said to be the first "post"-Christian, for whom "existing" Christianity is a mockery of the Evangelical ideal, for whom Christianity is not a given "belief" but *inexistent* unless testified by faith in it …

SO TOO YOU ARE THE FIRST "POST"-MARXIST TESTIFYING TO A CRITICALLY **INEXISTENT** MARXISM …

MAYBE SO. BUT MY FAITH IN MARXISM I PLACE IN THE REBELLIOUS COLONIZED. I ENDORSE FANON'S "EXISTENTIALISM" …

FOR THE NATIVE, LIFE CAN ONLY SPRING UP AGAIN OUT OF THE ROTTING CORPSE OF THE SETTLER.

The Wretched of the Earth (1961) by the militant psychiatrist in Algeria, **Frantz Fanon** (1925-61), was prefaced by Sartre: "to shoot down a European is to kill two birds with one stone, to destroy an oppressor and the man he oppresses at the same time: there remain a dead man and a free man; the survivor, for the first time, feels a *national* soil under his foot."

Sartre and Camus had by now come to bitter enmity, twice over. First, when Camus publicized his allergy to Marxism and all "revolutionary terror" in *The Rebel* (1952); and next, with his compromise position on Algerian independence – unpopular alike with Marxists, French colonists and Algerians – that French *pieds-noirs* settlers and native Algerians should co-exist in a federated "commonwealth". What would they say of the outcome today?

WHAT DID ALGERIA GAIN FROM INDEPENDENCE? MUCH BLOODSHED, FOLLOWED BY GOVERNMENTS OF ENDEMIC CORRUPTION, AND EVEN MORE BLOODSHED BY ISLAMIC FUNDAMENTALISTS ...

NO EXCUSE FOR DEFENDING COLONIALISM. UTOPIANS ARE THOSE WHO BELIEVE THAT SOMETHING BETTER CAN BE EXTRAPOLATED FROM A PRESENT THAT "MIGHT HAVE BEEN" BUT NEVER EXISTED.

The Existentialism that never was

I have imagined Sartre and Camus in "double take". Does history permit of repetition "recollected forwards" as Constantine Constantius inquires in his book, until disabled by a speck in the eye? My attempt to pinpoint the *when* of Existentialism is blunted – or goes out of focus as if by superimpositions of photographs taken at widely different times.

A vintage Existentialism

Existentialism does once appear memorable as in a vintage Brassaï photograph. Sartre accepted the label "existentialism", fabricated by its opponents, in 1944, and was thereupon enviably condemned for "terrifying nihilism" by two arch-reactionaries, the French Communist Party and Pope Pius XII in his encyclical *Humani generis* (1950). Existentialism was at once certified the proper attitude for the disaffected post-war youth – dark glasses, dark clothes, dark thoughts on despair and nothingness in dark smoke-filled jazz cellars …

Heidegger on parole

Irony ruled that Heidegger would be in the zone of French military occupation after Germany's defeat in 1945 – a suspect figure put under de-Nazification *Lehrverbot*, forbidden to teach until 1951. A reminder of Husserl's fate in 1935? Unlikely. Heidegger's "parole" and rehabilitation began with Sartre who had pronounced him "gutless" in 1944 and then interceded with the French authorities to have him invited to Paris. Heidegger's refuge is meanwhile his Todtnauberg "hut" in the Swabian Black Forest …

SARTRE? OH YES, THE FRENCHMAN WHO ALWAYS CONFUSED ME WITH HUSSERL …

Heidegger's *Letter on Humanism* (1949) rewards Sartre with its "sting in the tail" …

The sting in the tail

The fashionable scandal of Existentialism gave Sartre cause to defend its "austere technicalities" in his 1945 lecture "Existentialism is a Humanism". To this, Heidegger mordantly replied with his 1949 *Letter*. It is a densely veiled, *unrepentant* reclamation of Germany's philosophic destiny conjured by its last philosopher, **himself** – and *inter alia* proclaims surprisingly on Sartre's lack of *history* and *Marxism* …

HOMELESSNESS OF BEING IS ENTRENCHED IN THE **HISTORY OF METAPHYSICS** – SARTRE DOES NOT COMPREHEND THAT.

"Because Marx by experiencing estrangement attains an essential dimension of history, the Marxist view of history is superior to that of other historical accounts. But since neither Husserl nor – as far as I have seen till now – Sartre recognizes the essential importance of the *historical in being*, neither phenomenology nor existentialism enters that dimension within which a productive dialogue with Marxism first becomes possible."

Heidegger on endless parole

Thor is in the Vaucluse region of southern France: a sunlit idyll, men at a game of *pétanque*, a glass of *beaumes de Venise* – and Heidegger is there in the mid-1960s as a guest of the poet and former Resistance partisan **René Char** (1907-88). The Frenchman seems untroubled by Heidegger's Nazi episode. After leisurely discourses on Greek philosophy, they promenade by the river Sorgue.

Heidegger's enigmatic smile speaks volumes: *is it over …*

... is it over with Husserl?

Heidegger, cleansed of the Nazi tar-brush by a French intellectual élite, is explicable *intellectually* as their own domestic (con)fusion of phenomenology and Existentialism. Which explains nothing, really. Is he – as Hannah Arendt, former mistress of Heidegger in her student days, names him – "the secret king of thought" in our time? I see him rather as the cunning usurper Hagen in Wagner's *Ring Cycle*. Never mind that. Husserl hasn't quite given up the ghost …

A *sordino* theology

Mysterious nomenclature in Heidegger's *Being and Time* – "fallenness", "throwness", "anxiety" and other such disorientating terms – are unacknowledged retrievals from Kierkegaard's Christian existential categories. These are, so to speak, re-tempered by Heidegger to give an undertone music – a seductive *theologizing of phenomenology*. For instance: "Only if death, guilt, conscience, freedom, and finitude reside together equiprimordially in Being of an entity as they do in care, can that entity exist in the mode of fate; that is to say, only then can it be historical in the very depths of its existence."

HOW **MIGHT** I INTERPRET THAT PASSAGE?

AS THEOLOGY PLAYED **SORDINO**, "MUTE", FROM THE LATIN **SURDUS**, AS IN **ABSURDUS** – THE ABSURD.

Preaching the futural

It is pessimist theology that need not speak its name. Heidegger leaves Being "ajar" to existential Christianity as against Sartre's closure to it. Nowhere in *Being and Time* is "belief in God" *actual* but invites a twilight reading of absurd post-Christian transcendence, a susurration, a whispering to those in modern times deafened by the "death of God". Heidegger speaks with messianic zeal of Dasein's, i.e. man's, essentially *futural* destiny for "its time" …

DASEIN — THROWN INTO ITS **DA** ("THERE") OF **SEIN** (BEING) — IS FREE FOR DEATH AND SHATTERS AGAINST IT — AND IN A MOMENT OF FUTURAL VISION CLAIMS ITS TIME …

HE PREACHES A MYSTIC FUTURAL OF BEING — IN "ITS TIME" **NOW** OR IN THE **BEYOND**?

No wonder that modernist theologians of the German school like **Paul Tillich** (1886-1965) and **Rudolf Bultmann** (1884-1976) have espied in Heidegger an existential faith of "ultimate concern" in our time of unfaith. A French school of Catholicism transfused phenomenology, intermingled with Heideggerianism, into the sclerotic veins of orthodox Thomist theology to produce a temporary "existentialist" flush in the cheeks. Catholic existentialism, as espoused by **Gabriel Marcel** (1889-1973), did not withstand Pius XII's denunciation.

Perhaps by accident ...

Is there a Christian Existentialism? I answer only for myself in *preferring* an experience that speaks directly of *noche obscura*, "dark night of the soul", in the poetry of the Spanish mystic **St John of the Cross** (1542-91). Or in the poetry of that ailing, derelict being in a Jesuit's cassock, **Gerard Manley Hopkins** (1844-89), whose gaze on nature rewarded him with two words of astonishment: **inscape** – a sensation of "oneness" in the design of things which by piercing blaze of **instress** reveals them shining forth in Being. Is it an immanent force *in* nature he describes or a transcendent *supra*-evidence of God? Does it matter so long as I could see with his instructed eye?

In a diary entry of 18 May 1872, Hopkins sketches the inscaped head of a bluebell

"arched down like a cutwater drawing itself back from the line of the keel. The lines of the bell strike and overlie this, rayed but not symmetrically, some lie parallel ..."

25 August 1872. *This skeleton inscape of a spray-end of ash tree I broke at Wimbledon that summer is worth noticing for the suggested globe: it is leaf on the left and keys on the right.*

8 Sept. 1872. *I took my vows.*

I think this is phenomenology. Even, or particularly, in that laconic entry – "I took my vows" – those of a novice Jesuit. A lifelong vocation to witnessing Being.

What good besides to mention that Hopkins *preferred* the subtler theologian **Duns Scotus** (c. 1266-1308) to the Jesuits' officially "Thomist" one, **St Thomas Aquinas** (c. 1225-74)? That in Scotus he found the "principle of Individuation", *haecceitas*, "Thisness", which confirmed his sense of inscape and instress? And that Heidegger, product of a Jesuit-founded seminary, wrote his doctoral thesis on Duns Scotus?

Does it say, *by accident*, there is Christian Existentialism?

A return to fulfilled scepticism

Husserl's *science* of phenomenology cannot rest content with a naïve "God-created" world. The real enigma is that of consciousness *in* and *for* which a world becomes known. Only as *meant by us*, and from nowhere else, does the world, and we in it, gain meaning and validity. The problem then remains *scepticism* – unresolved rather than fulfilled – glossed over by Sartre's flight to systematized Marxism; while for Heidegger, scepticism is merely Dasein's "suicide" in face of indeterminate truth.

WHY DID BERKELEY IMPISHLY PICK HOLES IN REASON?

OF COURSE, HE WAS **BISHOP OF CLOYNE** – DEFENDER OF RELIGION'S TRANSCENDENT MYSTERIES. KIERKEGAARD MINUS THE ANGUISH!

The grey breath of reasoning

Berkeley didn't have Hegel's totalitarian system to confront. Nor did he need Kierkegaard's problem to see the "existential" predicament of faith threatened by the Enlightenment's rationalist empiricism. Nor did he need accept that reflection on the world "dries up" its immediacy into cold grey – an *anxiety* imputed by Kierkegaard for the absurdist "faith *problem*" (in Greek, pro-*bollo*, "throw forward") that gives Heidegger his "thrownness" into the futural.

For reasons of history

Three prisoners awaiting death are offered freedom if they can solve a puzzle. They are shown five discs – three white, two black – from which each prisoner will receive one of unknown colour pinned to his back. They are left in an empty room to contemplate each other in silence for an indefinite time. Whoever is first able to explain by logic and not by guesswork what colour he wears on his back will at once be released.

What this infernal puzzle really concerns is a *narrowing of vocabulary* at stake for my three antagonists.

Words of reckoning

I go back to 1933 and Sartre's assertion of "influences, oppositions, surpassings etc." that ensue from Husserl to Heidegger to an unnameable Existentialism. In close confinement, as in Sartre's play *Huis clos* (1944) wherein it is said "hell is other people" – their gaze is fixated on each other's similarities and discords in the unreal "now" which is only ever real and extendable in eternity. In reality, they take positions in recoil from one another, all for *reasons of history*.

I overhear their differences but undergo their resemblances.

A reduction to absolute existence

For whom is reality *meant*? Who else if not intended by us? Consciousness alone is not *preceded* by being meant but is itself the original of meaning. Such is Husserl's position. Indubitability is meaning for him, but to ascertain *how* it is so demands something absolute – ego reduced to its pure essence. "Only subjectivity can be 'for-itself' in a genuine and absolute way."

Existence need not be

Consciousness is an irreality that Heidegger fills in with Dasein, i.e. ordinary human being-thereness. Irreality nevertheless trails after Dasein in the sense Heidegger gives to its existence as a mode – a possibility *only* – of being or not-being authentic. Mode signifies a form that existence might substantially take or not – a "could be otherwise", or, in short, contingency. Authenticity is not (as often believed) Heidegger's ethical injunction but a question of Dasein's historical fate. What is that fate?

EXISTENCE IS NOT AN UNCONDITIONAL FACT OF BEING HUMAN. RATHER, IT IS **FROM BEING** THAT HUMAN **IS** ... AND THIS **NEED NOT BE**.

Being is history

Being is that which *happens to us*. It is no passive "thing" that we can presume essentially grasped in "things-in-being". Being is instead active self-determining proof from which we are, so to speak, protruded as "something other" in the midst of beings other than human. We are free on peril to secede from Being and reckon only on things-in-being as matters of our own doing. Inauthenticity will thereupon take form as *inexistence* become *unrecognizable to itself*.

What hope of human still "being"?

Being is not eternal but a gift to us *limited by time*. Being itself, not we, will determine the "fate of things" as it recedes from our history of technicized progress. Oblivion is the name that Heidegger gives to that history which – in his astounding conception of it – is nothing other than *metaphysics* as the essential history of human being. Heidegger does follow on the question of "crisis" in science preoccupying Husserl but as history foreclosing on an inescapable trinity: metaphysics = science = technology. Metaphysics does not vanish with technology but gains its final form of dominant *event* …

… THE **FORGETTING** OF BEING WHICH STARTS WITH ITS APPROPRIATION BY "SCIENTIFIC TRUTH" IN PHILOSOPHY ITSELF SINCE PLATO'S TIME.

Being and recession to nihilism

We succeed from one thing to another – probing deep space, cracking the genetic code at full speed to manifesting the truths of *every*thing. Does the essence of human *being* consist in its scientific explanation? We are inclined to say yes and meanwhile succumb to nihilism. Nihilism resides bewilderingly in *positive value* which entrusts sole validity to our mastery of things. Opposition to it is denied thought. (Techno-) logic gives the illusion of entering straightforwardly into thinking when it is in fact being disavowed. No "offensive" against science is thinkable because its power is what philosophy has completely dissolved itself *into*.

Salvation from the thing

In a manuscript note of 1910, Husserl laments a chronic error of empiricism: "Consciousness … is not a psychical experience, not a network of psychical experiences, not a thing, not an appendage (state, action) to a natural object. Who will save us from the *reification* of consciousness? He would be the saviour of philosophy …". Reification is to treat as a "thing" what isn't one: an abstract entity transmuted into object. Heidegger in *Being and Time* scoffs at Husserl's worry and questions why the "reifying" of consciousness keeps coming back to exercise its domination.

A purge for nausea

Sartre evinces a pathological disgust for the glutinous turgidity of things. Roquentin, the anti-hero of his novel *Nausea* (1938), sickens at the feel of a moist pebble – what in *Being and Nothingness* is named the opaqueness of unconscious reality's being-in-itself. Husserl's consciousness for-itself impressed Sartre as a relief – a translucent gap of nothingness – that appears in compact in-itselfness and makes all the difference between being human and being thing.

Epochē distils a pure transcendental "I" from consciousness given in its natural (or immanent) attitude. Consciousness must divest itself of naïve empirical self-experience to arrive at that "unnatural, inhuman" absolute ego. Sartre also reverses this crucial Husserlian tenet. He dispenses altogether with *epochē*, so that ego – instead of being Husserl's identical pole of all our conscious acts – is now constituted by a transcendental act of consciousness. Only consciousness is permitted *existential* transcendence from the immanent "staying put" of material reality. Ego is itself suspect of thingness – indeed Sartre calls it an "opaque blade" which threatens death to the lucidity of consciousness.

Acts of nihilation

Nothingness is not the Husserlian "irreality" of reduced pure ego but, for Sartre, those "irrealizations" accomplished by acts of consciousness. He means those absences or negativities by which consciousness perforates the impermeable compactness of Being-in-itself and allows us to imagine things otherwise than they are. Negativity gives a free space of "maybe" to our projects of change. An example: if Sartre expects Simone at the Café de Flore but she doesn't appear, that place then becomes *where she isn't*. Everything *there* serves as reference to the absence *she is* …

A conscious pact of freedom

Sartre's concern is for absolute freedom which can only be in consciousness emancipated from the world of *things caused*. Whatever else, "I am" is otherwise existentially situated in that world of causal limits. Consciousness alone is pure free spontaneity, transcendental in the sense of being *impersonal*: "every moment of our conscious life reveals to us a creation out of nothing". Consciousness dissolves its I-owner into a ceaseless stream of such creations "out of nothing". No self therefore enjoys priority over others equally constituted by that same impersonal stream of consciousness.

A lack of being

I ask myself: why this paranoid resistance to "thingness" in Sartre?
I must first recognize that "I" – that illusory thing "I am" – is a falling-off
from consciousness to existence. Existence is the I-situation of consciousness in the world. What is consciousness then faced with? Its
own anguishing "not" of possibility – its own freedom to choose being
this or that – which means freedom in effect is *lack of being* that must
feed on material in-itselfness. At risk to its lucidity, consciousness as
lack will seek being in material plenitude that *resists* and yet *commands*
us in our situation.

"Existence precedes essence"

This is Sartre's classic slogan of Existentialism. It is axiomatic of his arm's-length hygiene against things. I can follow the steps … If consciousness is only there *impersonally* by transparent acts of nihilation; if existence is the situation of consciousness condemned in its lack of being to the world; then essence is an appetite of for-itself possibly being *something* in-itself, indeed, a temptation to absolute gluttony of "wanting to be God" as the for-itself-in-itself …

Freedom is without history

Sartre's pessimism gives way to realizing that human desire for the "unlimited" is not a useless passion but a condition of history. The fullness of being-in-itself – matter "as such" – is never encountered devoid of human significance. What is there for us materially is conditioned by our productive activity – and by *scarcity*. Precisely that – a Darwinian struggle over scarce resources – will determine the limits on what any human can be in a class system of productivity. Liberation from sordid oppressive "thingness" brings Sartre inevitably to Marxism which is "history itself become consciousness of itself" ...

The ecstasy of time

Heidegger deplores Sartre's conception of existence as one more relapse into metaphysics. "Existence precedes essence" is Sartre's wrongful understanding of Heidegger's assertion in *Being and Time*: "The essence of Dasein lies in its existence." Fatally wrong in Heidegger's eyes. Existence is not in human *doing* but in closeness to the source that determines its being – its *ek-sistence* – existence reinstated in nearness to "ecstasy". What is gained by Heidegger's neologism "ek-sistence"? And what affinity does it have to "ecstasy" which in Greek means to be "placed" out of one's senses?

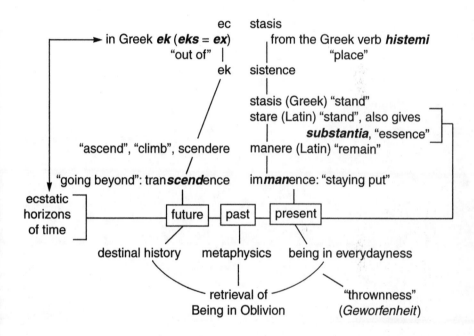

"The essence of Dasein lies in its existence" also has for Heidegger the sense of "The 'substance' of the human being is ek-sistence". We can see that "essence" derives from the Latin *stare* which is the root of "substance". Substance in Greek is *ousia* as a "state of being". Heidegger is well-aware that *parousia*, as the affined noun of *ousia*, means the present as a *waiting-towards* (the future) to which Christian eschatology gives the sense of Second Advent of Christ. So, then, is Heidegger saying: time is the ecstatic "substance" of human beings?

A draught from the well

What is human being in "ecstasy" for? The answer is dazzlingly simple: for its essence *in time*. Which is to say even simpler that human essence is *not known* to it. Essence is the "yet" of suspense. Will we be "in time" to know our essence? The ambiguity is glaring – not only of time running out for us but of somehow not being *in it*. To ek-sist ec-statically unambiguously states that for a time Dasein "stands in the clearing of Being" …

The redeeming Advent

Once again I am instructed that Being has its own "destinal" unfolding history, in which Dasein's "being there" at all is determined in its essence. Time is therefore substantially *that* history and *no other*. But, if that is so, our usual temporal "horizons" of past, present and future cannot be what they commonly seem for us – a flowing succession of "nows" in being. Time can of course simply appear to pass. But in our proper ecstatic condition, time is *advent*, a future being sent to us.

Time talk ...

Concerning time, there is nothing to say. Or too much. We are always talking time – how it "drags" or "flies", "where does it go?", "profit" from it or "waste" it – how differently it ebbs from us in boredom, anxiety or everyday slippage – uncanny in déjà-vu, unreliable in forecast, or imagined cyclical – inconstant yet permanent, always we are enslaved by "it". How can time be a *substance somehow* determining for us?

The time-partials of consciousness

Time "is" only by consciousness of it. Time fields are constituted by absolute consciousness whose originary presence is not itself a modality of time. Husserl does not say time is "made up" by us but rather is *intuitionally* absolute – it *would be* even if consciousness were not. However, consciousness is itself partialized by *Abschattungen*, profiles or horizons, only one of which will be actual – the "now" – and others past or still future. The problem is "consciousness of the *now* is not itself *now*". Now cannot emerge from itself; it has no graspable "profile"-content in itself …

The retained slipping-away

What is Husserl saying? That I can have an impression of the momentary as actual *when it is not?* I do, in fact, because consciousness is characterized by being *already there* before becoming an object of my (self-)perception. It is precisely this originary *retentional* past in consciousness that allows both my *impressional* "nowness" and my futural *protention* – a "stretching forwards" (from the Latin (pro)*tendere*) to my intuitive anticipation of the whole. These are the three time-horizons of intentionality ...

The socially partial horizons

Husserl is accused of insensitivity to the existential vicissitudes of being in the world which Heidegger and Sartre anatomize. He reduces the person to a likeness of the disembodied "observer" in theoretical physics.

HUSSERL SEEMS ONLY TO REQUIRE OF AN "I" THAT IT UNDERSTAND **SOMETHING** ...

HE ABRIDGES "I" OF ALL ITS QUALITIES — AGE, SEX, ETHNICITY, ENVIRONMENT AND HISTORY — AN "I" WITHOUT BIOGRAPHY.

A MISTAKEN VIEW OF HUSSERL'S CONCERN ...

THE SUBJECT'S EXISTENTIAL CONDITIONS ARE RELATIVE TO A FREEDOM EARNED BY ALWAYS KNOWING "**I CAN DO OTHERWISE ...**"

But we are most often the unknowing hostages of *socially partial* horizons – gender, race, milieu and so on – the *Abschattungen* determined by our natural attitude to them.

Über allen Gipfeln
Ist Ruh

"Over the peaks lies peace ..." begins a poem by **J.W. von Goethe** (1749-1832). A human skyline is traced in those words, as I find also in these by the French poet **Jacques Dupin** (b. 1927): "Ever since my fears came of age, the mountain has needed me. Has needed my chasms, my bonds, my step." It is not the chasm that "gives" me vertigo but I who invest it with "fearsome depth" that it doesn't possess. Nor do the peaks have "peace" without my bestowal of it.

ALL BARRIERS TO VERTIGO GIVE WAY IN MY CONSCIOUSNESS OF FREEDOM ...

"POETICALLY DWELLS MAN ON THIS EARTH", SAYS HÖLDERLIN ...

I UNDERSTAND THE UNNATURALNESS OF EPOCHÉ: WE ARE NOT EXPECTED BY REALITY ...

The moment of history

"Unexpected by reality" – is that not our *history*? What is history? That which can be otherwise but never is. Total pessimism would say: that which happens to us and about which we can do nothing. And yet, self-evidently, there is *change*. But it is an absurd change that flows *exactly as it flows*. We are hostage to the change that we ourselves make, consciously or not. Does it have exit – as Sartre hopes into freedom; or into Dasein's redeeming "ecstasy", for Heidegger?

Heidegger's *Mein Kampf*

Heidegger never disavowed his deep belief that to him alone was granted a mystical vision of "the inward truth and greatness" of the Nazi movement. He arose from humble origins, the sexton's son from Messkirch, striving mightily and yearning always for highest status in the German academic aristocracy. His moment dawned in 1933, when he felt his own and Germany's world mission had decisively intertwined, and he plunged as *Führer-Rektor* of Freiburg University into full implementation of the Nazi *Gleichschaltung* programme. There is no doubt of Heidegger's ambition – to be appointed *spiritual guide* of National Socialism, the Nazi "Hegel".

Rassengedanke: racial thought

Heidegger's abstruse academic version of Nazism – which "speaks Greek" – made him suspect to plebeian Nazi officialdom. Party spies monitored his lectures – and it was in a series of these on Nietzsche (1936-40) that Heidegger alleged his *resistance* to Nazism. What resistance is it, on the eve of full-scale genocide, to "think race" for his students?

I AM EXPLORING THE **ENDING** OF METAPHYSICS IN NIETZSCHE, NOT ADVOCATING RACIALISM.

"Only where the absolute subjectivity of will to power comes to be the truth of beings as a whole is the *principle* of a programme of racial breeding possible ... in terms of the self-conscious *thought* of race. That is to say, the principle is metaphysically necessary. Just as Nietzsche's thought of will to power was ontological rather than biological, even more was his racial thought metaphysical rather than biological in meaning."

A prophecy from Germany

Why choose Nietzsche as oppositional model at the moment of Heidegger's "inner emigration" from "vulgar" Nazism? Heidegger sees very well that Nietzsche cannot be *displaced* from Germany's enigma, i.e., Hitler as the actuary of Nietzsche's Will to Power. Nietzsche thinks the "blond beast" and – as Heidegger rightly says – "ends" metaphysics by placing the Cartesian ego at the service of animality. A risky thought *calculative of power* is enacted by Hitler's troglodyte opera, *The Triumph of the Will*, visible to the entire world.

The crisis of modernity

Karl Jaspers canonized Nietzsche along with Kierkegaard as the founding saints of Existentialism. An absurdity little better than claiming him a postmodernist. Nietzsche is to be strictly aligned with the *crisis* of modernity – decadence, nihilism and aestheticized politics. "Atheism" for him, as for Kierkegaard, is the *actual state* of pious hypocrisy in a de-Christianized society. Its secular religion is democracy – a final descent to nihilism, a levelling to anonymous statistical man with no values but its own mass abstraction.

DARWIN GIVES US A FOOL'S EVOLUTION FOR THE SUCCESS ONLY OF INFERIOR **MASS EXISTENCES** – FINE FOR BACTERIA AND COCKROACHES BUT NOT FOR US.

MERE NUMERICAL PROLIFERATION IS NOT FOR MAN. WE ARE DISTINGUISHED BY METAPHYSICAL **BREEDING** ...

Will to Power as art

Nietzsche is irrecuperably anti-democratic, no doubt, but what is he really about? He is the thinker of post-Darwinian catastrophe, aware that evolution by random mutation leaves everything in a nihilist state of *designless fluidity*. What value has the species man if in principle it is liable to *replacement* – but by *what*? The overcoming of man by the *Übermensch*, by "super"- or "supra"-man, is the occulted meaning of "God is dead". It means the struggle for self-elected quality – by Will to Power as art – which redeems only the few from blind species mass-existence.

148

The rising star

Heidegger's ambition is too lofty for confinement to anti-Semitism or racialist eugenics. It is not resistance to that programme of Nazism he seeks in Nietzsche but rather a replacement to Husserl's thought on crisis in science. Nietzsche is first hailed in Heidegger's Rectoral Address of 1933 as Germany's "last philosopher" who thinks the crisis of modern man's "forsakenness in the midst of things-in-being". Nietzsche is Heidegger's means of taking "the inward truth and greatness" of Nazism into his refuge of "inner emigration" and from there to summons the historical unfolding of Being as such.

The poverty of repentance

Heidegger issues summonses to penitence from his Todtnauberg forest hut. Dasein as mere "caretaker" of Being must regain its "essential poverty of the shepherd". Of his own repentance, nothing is said, not a word ever offered on the Holocaust. He will publicly lament the sufferings of Germany's soldiers – indeed, a careful indiscretion in his 1949 *Letter* makes this plain enough. "When confronted with death, therefore, those young Germans who knew about Hölderlin lived and thought something other than what the public held to be the typical German attitude."

A word in the heart

Karl Löwith's puzzlement in Rome in 1936 transfers more gravely to the poet of the Holocaust, **Paul Celan** (1920-70). It may seem inscrutable to us that Celan, a Jew tormented by his own survival, would feel deep sympathy for Heidegger's thought. Celan's poem "Todtnauberg" (1970) commemorates a three-day visit to Heidegger in 1967. He notes the "starred die" above the well, signs the guest-book, inscribing it with a line …

a hope, today,
of a thinking man's
coming
word
in the heart …

No word ever came, of course. Celan in Paris, April 1970, commits suicide by drowning.

The right to remain silent

That right belongs only to survivors of the Holocaust whose life *after it* is unimaginable to us. I emphasize after the ordeal, not during what was literally unspeakable. Celan's poetry – a stark denuded German truly in penitence – does speak in terrifying exception to what lacks any equivalent in words. Heidegger has no right to a silence which – on his own terms of the *forgotten* "unspoken word of being" – makes him blameworthy of Celan's death. His parole ends as ex-engineer Kirilov steps out from the trees, and …

THERE IS A STAR ON HEIDEGGER'S GRAVESTONE IN MESSKIRCH CHURCHYARD …

Existentialism without illusions

Murder is not, even when fictitious, a proper philosophic response. I know. As I also know that *Being and Time* is still my favourite bedside book of suicide. I am in no illusion when often I find myself in agreement with Heidegger; but his *rightness* confuses me, as apparently it does not for some of his apologists. Is existential thinking compatible with fascism, which for Sartre is that rock-like inhumanity impervious to ever thinking itself mistaken? Is that Heidegger's *compactness* of silence?

Speaking of deception

Deception is always possible by the *negativity* of free consciousness. Simply, I have the choice of lying to you. The lie is proof that consciousness exists *undeceived* in me – by nature of its hidden intention from you; and exists for you – by an undetected absence of truth. The liar does not exist in the consciousness of his lie, unless he falls victim to it. And here the impossible problem of *self*-deception begins. Impossible because – given the total translucency of consciousness – how can I lie to myself without seeing through it at once?

HOW CAN I CONSCIOUSLY **INTEND** TO HIDE THE TRUTH FROM MYSELF?

IT SEEMS IN THE NATURE OF BEING FOR-MYSELF THAT I HAVE THE CHOICE OF DENYING MYSELF ...

Self-deception is of course subject to instability, a re-awakening to good faith or cynicism in awareness of one's performance. Look at the café waiter in his superb automaton ballet. He is performing the thing-in-itself of *waiter* that he himself and others expect of a waiter. He is what he *is not* – a "thing that serves" – and exactly this peculiar "not" of consciousness threatens it always with self-deception.

155

A schism in consciousness

Freud neatly resolves the problem of unaware self-deception by cutting psychic life into conscious "ego" and unconscious "id". I stand as ego in no privileged position of knowledge to "it" (*id* in Latin) but like someone vulnerable to a deceiver's lie. There is *truth* in the id's deception whose purpose is unknown to me but which, if I could reattach it to my conscious reality, would be my *entire* truth. But that is the id's inadmissibly unpleasant or illicit truth unconsciously repressed and *mis*represented to me in disguise as a "complex".

This idea is illustrated by a story in Freud's *Psychopathology of Everyday Life* (1901).

Freud travels with a young Jewish academic who bemoans the fate of his people "doomed to atrophy" by racial prejudice. He attempts an impassioned plea in Latin from Virgil's *Aeneid*: "Let someone arise from bones as an avenger!", but gets it wrong and forgets the word for "someone", *aliquis*. Freud is enlisted to explain why that pronoun slipped into unconsciousness …

He admits to an affair with an Italian woman whose periods have stopped, which signals an unwelcome pregnancy.

A lie without a liar

Why should a worrying pregnancy censor the word *aliquis*? Freud's explanation is that the young man's wish is for a descendant "to avenge him" but a Jewish one is not *thinkable* from "someone" Gentile. His wish is therefore repudiated and "blocked" from memory. Sartre's objection is that a censorship of memory implies *awareness* at some level of the thing repressed. How else could Freud's questions possibly aim at the subject's comprehension? The censor must be aware of what it chooses not to be conscious of, in short, it is in self-deception.

Is there undeceived choice?

A young student of Sartre came to him with a dilemma – whether to join the Resistance and avenge his brother killed in the German offensive of 1940, or look after his afflicted mother whose only consolation is in him. Either way, his choice would have legitimate reasons. But, as Sartre reminds him, "no rule of general morality can show you what you ought to do."

Choice is *non-foundational*: it "only is" by enclosure in its other – *no choice*.

Solipsism or intersubjectivity?

The capacity of consciousness to deceive others and itself is already implied if not explored by Husserlian phenomenology. What else is the *natural attitude* – that supposition of reality's pre-givenness – but the immanent ground of our deception in its ever-presentness? Reduction by *epochē* undeceives us but at the cost of unnaturalness. Moreover, does not *epochē*'s proof of absolute ego result in pure *solipsism*?

Falling into "theyness"

Husserl inclines to an optimistic view of our intersubjective world; but he also knows it is an incubator of isolated monads whose intentions are deceptively hidden from each other. Heidegger recognizes self-deception as Dasein's existentially determinative "falling" (*Verfallen*) into irresponsible "theyness": "The *'they'*, which supplies the answer to the question of the *'who'* of everyday Dasein, is the *'nobody'* to whom every Dasein has already surrendered himself in being-among-one-another."

Being among one another

Dasein's falling into neuter "theyness" is malignant intersubjectivity. Heidegger insists it is not a moral judgement but a simple fact of being in the world. "The 'they' can … be answerable for everything most easily, because it is not someone who needs to vouch for anything. It 'was' always the 'they' who did it, and yet it can be said that it has been 'no one'." Heidegger in 1927 anticipates not only "corporate man" but the advance of Nazism's mass rank-and-file …

Being for-others in Sartre's regard has that same glutinous proximity of *thingness* – a distasteful coercion. "Hell is others." Others who enter my field of perception rob me of it – my gaze is "raped" by their look whose meaning bewilders me. Others are indispensable to my existence but their presence threatens mine with malign uncertainties. Sartre is left with *inexistent* Marxism to gain freedom from history; just as Heidegger relies on the "uncanniness" of Being to redeem Dasein from deterioration to thing-in-being.

I AM BY **NECESSITY OF OTHERS**? THIS WILL NOT DO FOR THE SPITEFUL MAN OF THE UNDERGROUND ...

WHAT DO I CARE FOR OTHERS' SIMILARITY TO ME? I DESPISE MY IGNORANCE, BUT EVEN MORE THOSE WHO SHARE IT.

Do we hide from ourselves a grudge against existence? Is it there, a sickness apparent in the quarantine of others' gaze? Husserl dignifies it with the name scepticism – that by which the natural attitude seeks to undeceive itself by suicidal reductionism. In the event, philosophy secedes entirely to psychology. Husserl's *bête noire* is "psychologism": truth dependent on contingent functionings of mind. He opposes its founders, Locke, Berkeley and Hume, with his conviction that mental-ized sense-data are not what human consciousness shares in common but *only* the natural attitude itself.

> I LIKE ANCHOVIES, YOU DON'T – THAT TRUTH IS NATURALLY GIVEN. I CANNOT EMPIRICALLY INSPECT IT.

> WHAT OF OTHER **CONTINGENCIES** – IS THE COLOUR "ORANGE" ESSENTIAL TO THE BEING OF AN ORANGE?

How can I know the essence "red" from all the contingencies of redness – coagulated blood, a glass of claret, a sunset, Van Gogh's hair …?

How can we experience a *same* world differentiated in each one of us by partial solipsism? Does a mood or a pain change "what is" or only my relation to it? In either case, my mood is not the same as yours in its coloration of reality. Emotions, in Sartre's view, are *degradations* of consciousness by which I try to reach my objective magically in transcendent flight from reality – that is, in *bad faith*.

I CALL THIS DASEIN IN **FACTICITY**, "AT LOSS" AMONG THINGS.

BEING "AT LOSS" IS ITS OWN PURPOSIVE BEHAVIOUR WHICH, IF PURIFIED OF BAD FAITH BY REFLECTION, IS NOT FATAL TO FREEDOM.

YOU MISS SOMETHING ... CONSCIOUSNESS FINALLY REDUCED TO **ARTIFICIAL** DECEPTION.

The Turing Test

The pioneer of computerology **Alan Turing** (1912-54) devised a "blindfold" test in which a human subject must attempt to establish by questions whether the respondent screened off from view is another human or a computer. A computer whose responses pass as human can be said successfully to emulate intellect.

What advance on consciousness is that to assume it answered by deceiving it?

Artificial intelligence is our own self-deception based on an unjustified presupposition of consciousness.

The new superstition

Turing's "deception" is a final stage in psychologistic scepticism that began with Descartes' *res cogitans*, the "thinking substance", now become "thinking machine". Husserl already stated in 1900 that logical laws are not inferable from psychological "matter of fact" states. If human thought is an epiphenomenon or by-product of neural materiality – how do we *know* this? How does "thought" escape from causal closure in matter? Or, more simply, how can matter possibly give rise to the *idea* of matter?

UNLESS WE ARE SAYING THAT MATTER IN ITSELF EXPRESSES "REASONS" TO WHICH OUR THOUGHT CORRESPONDS ...

AN ABSURDITY THAT IS INEVITABLE FOR PSYCHOLOGISM'S "THINKING SUBSTANCE".

What does Husserl mean by "psychologism"? He has in mind the aim of all "depth psychology" – whether clinical or experimental – to theorize consciousness as a mere stratum or derivative of biology. It would appear that empirical procedures can arrive at the true essential dynamics of life by omitting consciousness altogether. Such an omission has occurred because consciousness was always assumed – in its "immediate pregivenness" – as nothing that in itself needs explaining. And so we have progressed "deeper" – into Freudian mechanism of libidinal instincts; and, finally deepest, to a genetic status of "mind" whose very existence is presumed quantifiable by degrees of intelligent *performance* ...

Transubstantiated performance

We no longer have to keep faith with the body's original qualities. It now seems we are empowered to short-circuit the long-term random effects of natural selection by immediate recourse to cultural – and I would add, *psychological* – selection.

Gene test can screen embryos for low IQ

Lois Rogers
Medical Correspondent

SCIENTISTS have developed a £125 test that enables doctors to screen embryos for low intelligence. Their testing kit can identify a range of genetic defects known to lead to learning difficulties.

Developed by a British company, it is the first gene test for low IQ and has already been adapted for use by doctors in America and Spain on families they suspect have an inherited risk of a defect.

Using test-tube baby techniques, the American and Spanish doctors have selected only perfect embryos to be returned to the womb.

Some experts are concerned that such testing echoes Aldous Huxley's Brave New World, in which epsilon babies were bred in hatcheries for menial tasks while alphas lived a life of luxury.

"There is an urgent need for regulation of what constitutes legitimate use of this type of genetic diagnosis," said Richard Nicholson, the editor of the Bulletin of Medical Ethics.

"Low IQ is not life-threaten-ing. This is a significant step towards eugenics."

The £125 kit being marketed by Cytocell, of Banbury, was developed from research at the Institute of Molecular Medicine, Oxford.

Scientists have identified the specific arrangements of genetic material on the telomeres, the ends of DNA strands in each chromosome, which cause children to suffer anything from moderate learning problems to mental handicap.

About 21,000 children are born with a learning difficulty in Britain each year. Scientists say the test could identify up to 2,000 of them.

Research is now turning to the quest for other genetic characteristics which may cause sub-normal intelligence, with the ultimate goal of offering screening to women carrying naturally conceived babies.

Cytocell has already produced customised probes for couples at high risk of having mentally retarded children at the St Barnabas Medical Centre in New Jersey and at a genetics centre in Barcelona.

The American government is ploughing federal funds into developing such tests.

Because it is possible ...

Who would want to photograph this? The question lies hidden in what I am made to see. And what do I see? A mother shielding her child. I cannot see the child she protects from the gunman. The photographer has unknowingly affirmed a victory. A mother's protectiveness will always stand for life itself. She is monumentally the victor.

I now ask myself: what is hidden from us in a being *not yet* in this world? Who would want to gene-test its IQ? What does gene-testing say for us?

"I prefer an intelligent child, *naturally* ..." The natural attitude surrenders regularly to the fact of what is done. It does not provide for its own *unimaginableness*. Heidegger's warning is right: "to have had the thought of what technology *might* do is already the *event* of its doing."

Is it too late to redeem the natural attitude from its state of history?

Notes on a nameless philosophy

"It's the end of the world," the optimist despairs.
"No it isn't," replies the pessimist.

It has always been "too late" for us. But perhaps Existentialism is appointed precisely for too-lateness, at the last minute before it. *What is Existentialism, then?*

There is an unidentified *convergence* in my trio's antagonism, a philosophy as yet nameless. I could name it existential phenomenology originally scheduled by Husserl from which Heidegger and Sartre "deviated". But that is not accurately the focus. Heidegger and Sartre do not say better "a philosophy relevant to life" than Husserl. Something that "needs saying" is not necessarily a "saying better" than the original equity from which is drawn the possibility of saying.

This is hard to grasp but crucial if Existentialism gives any promise of rescue from a postmodern ideology of relativism. Existentialism is a "false memory syndrome" but of philosophy itself awaiting its interminable recovery from scepticism.

The greatest enemy of philosophy in Husserl's eyes are those philosophers who *have* "a philosophy" – one indeed that has resolved all its problems by running out of them. True philosophers are the "functionaries" of a "state of philosophy" in which humanity's direction of the will is manifested. What is that direction? Towards ever greater sci-entific objectivity which is in peril of forgetfulness that its origin is nowhere else than in the life-world of subjectivity. How are we to realize that science is nothing other than a *directive* from that total life-world? It cannot be grasped at all merely by a sense of "intensifying crisis" that science seems to bring to "life". We experience the problem – but the wrong way round. Why is that? Because the life-world is not accessible to a person in the natural attitude which has entirely fallen spellbound to science. To break that spell requires a suspension of science – an effort of *epochē* which is by no means a lapse into irrationalism – to catch sight of pure subjectivity in all its life-world horizons.

Redemption of the natural attitude is Husserl's fundamental question, answered by the wonder of consciousness. Heidegger's "ecstatical" Dasein in the midst of things-in-being; Sartre's *realité humaine* of consciousness in a permanent state of choice – am I wrong to see in them a narrowing of the gap of difference? What brings them nearer is a baneful consensus of urgency – is it too late to redeem our state of history? Husserl's ghost may be replaced by the spectre of Marx for Sartre, or Nietzsche's for Heidegger – but what does that matter anymore to a history which is *over* for us?

Moral facticity

The interesting fact is this. A *logician* – Edmund Husserl – demands a return to living experience. Why is that interesting? Did not another logician, also with a real vocation, **Ludwig Wittgenstein** (1889-1951), urge exactly the same? He did, but for him philosophy is a "language illness", a "bewitchment by words" whose cure is in ordinary language use. Are we to be forbidden bewitching words like "consciousness", "intuition", "being" …? The problem malingers. There is no *undeceived* language: especially not the inappropriate seizure of language by logic that results in "intelligent" machines and our present condition of technologicized being.

Hume famously proposed that there are "no moral facts". That is unsustainable now when the moral has taken on the possible of fact, i.e., *facticity* in Descartes' original sense of made by us, artificial, virtual. Consider again the performative implications of gene-testing the IQ of an embryo. But suppose I chose not to test the future performance of my unborn child? That choice would not succeed to displace our greater dependence on technology's improvements in "quality of life". There are no moral eventualities in our present without end. Or so it looks *at present …*

Invitation to a warning

Essentialist questions are not existentialist ones. Essentialist are not only such questions as "Is there a God?" or "What is the meaning of life?" or others of a "humanist" nature, but even those of verifiable scientific consequence. For instance, Darwinian evolution by natural selection, or, more pressingly for us today, the "selfish gene" theory from which evolutionary psychology takes guidance. Does not such a genetic theory allege the priority of "randomness" over any essential meaning to life? Molecular biology appears to deprive life of customary meaning, but, in fact, by prescribing what life is "really about", it endows existence with its final inalienable essence.

This is my radical departure. Anything which seeks to impose essential meaning on existence should be unmasked as *literature*. It is dissembled literature whose motive is to subordinate consciousness to an imperceptible unconscious. A deception that must be refused.

There will always be minds who delight in belittling mind – who contrive machines that think "like us" or torment chimpanzees enough to communicate "like us". To what end? For a better reckoning of what consciousness is "like"? To censure human arrogance? The greatest arrogance is to inflict a disabling reduction on mind while at the same time exploiting mind's own complexity to practise that deceit.

Husserl meant by reduction what its Latin origin preserves for us – *re-ducere*, a "leading back" to an unlimited domain of experience. He asks that any scientific reduction must account for itself by reference to that expanded field of experience. For instance – explanations of consciousness by reduction to "neuro-circuitry" in cognitive science; or human behaviour reduced to "selfish gene" strategies in evolutionary psychology – are those explanations accounted for because cognitive science or evolutionary psychology reduce *inclusively* to them? In other words, any explanation by reduction must violate its own immanence to be intelligible – it must have something additionally "transcendent" that departs from the standpoint of pregivenness of which it is apparently sufficient explanation. The explanation cannot of course "explain itself". Evolutionary psychology or any other reductionist state of mind cannot say of itself that it is a perfect explanation of things as they are because of being in the same condition as they are – if so, it would "stay put" in its immanence not only unintelligible but unsayable.

Reductionists might answer that knowing about a particular determined situation is not the same as being under total dictatorship to it. But this too is a transcendent violation of immanence. "Transcendence" means something not *besides* the fact of the world but not *in* the world either.

Karl Popper (1902-94) introduced "falsifiability" as a vital test of scientific credibility. It is nevertheless an afterthought of logic and not first to the actual doing of science. We do not need a philosophy, as Heidegger says, that limps after science in the hope of discovering its "method". We need one that "runs ahead of it" in the exploration of being. But how is that exploration to proceed without orientation from *epochē*'s realized consciousness in being?

Husserlian *epochē* could prove a more vital existentialist test of science than any which tamely follow after it.

Perhaps then a nameless philosophy might gain the proper name of Existentialism.

Flight from meaning

Meaning is not a necessary provision for any philosophy, nameless or not. But it creeps back even into the senseless. Camus' vigilant absurdism is not immune to a "sense" of atheistic mysticism.

Meaning is not something we can ever "have", any more than we can deny or banish it. It is there – in the fatal gap between experience and reality. The question is how, in its distance from us, it returns.

Perhaps only in extreme suspension – in a temporary "invalidation of being" by *epochē* – does it blaze forth as the unexpected that overwhelms us for a moment. A vertigo, in fact, unbearable for too long.

So, is it that? The very thing we seem most to long for and pursue – meaning – is what we cannot bear? Is this only how we can take cognizance of meaning – as that which is most nightmarishly fearsome to us?

I DESIRE NO MORE THAN MY OWN HUMANITY PROVE ME WRONG.

Further Reading

I have raised questions in this book organically fitted to the uncertainties of the answers on Existentialism. Other questions might be asked that would yield different uncertainties.

I shall list those books from which my references chiefly derive. First perhaps I should mention a "classic" – **Walter Kaufmann**, *Existentialism from Dostoevsky to Sartre* (London: Thames and Hudson, 1957). This is an introductory anthology of texts by the main contenders, although I disagree with its literary bias.

Albert Camus, *The Myth of Sisyphus* (New York: Vintage Books, 1960). I begin with this short, readable book; but also worthwhile is *The Rebel* (New York: Vintage Books, 1960).

Jean-Paul Sartre, *Being and Nothingness*, trans. Hazel Barnes (London: Routledge, 1958). Lengthy and forbidding, but the chapter on "Existential Psychoanalysis" should be read. An important source for me is *Search for a Method*, trans. Hazel Barnes (New York: Vintage Books, 1968) – a brief, lucid and personal account of Sartre's own Marxist version of Existentialism.

Martin Heidegger, *Being and Time*, trans. J. Macquarrie and E. Robinson (New York: Harper & Row, 1962). Massively difficult, of course. I take my approach from "Letter on 'Humanism'" (1949), in M. Heidegger, *Pathways*, ed. W. McNeill (Cambridge: Cambridge University Press, 1998), a brief enough, digestible essay. Heidegger's "Letter" is in part a response to Sartre's 1945 lecture "Existentialism is a humanism" (usually entitled *Existentialism and Humanism* in English translations, e.g. London: Eyre Methuen Ltd., 1975) which should be read first.

Edmund Husserl. The only accessible introduction I can recommend is Herbert Spiegelberg, *The Phenomenological Movement*, 2 vols. (The Hague: Martinus Nijhoff, 1969), which also contains good accounts of Heidegger, Sartre, Gabriel Marcel and other phenomenologists. I have gained personally from two books of a more technical nature: Rudolf Bernet, I. Kern and E. Marbach, *An Introduction to Husserlian Phenomenology* (Illinois: Northwestern University Press, 1993); J.J. Kockelmans, *Edmund Husserl's Phenomenology* (Indiana: Purdue University Press, 1994). Husserl's difficulty is real, but also exaggerated – I suggest reading his *The Crisis of European Sciences and Transcendental Phenomenology*, trans. David Carr (Illinois: Northwestern University Press, 1970).

Karl Jaspers. Some will think me unfair to Jaspers. For a corrective appreciation, I suggest Hannah Arendt, *Men in Dark Times* (New York: Harcourt, Brace, Jovanovich, 1968) and Jaspers' own views in his essays contained in the Kaufmann anthology.

Søren Kierkegaard, *Repetition*, trans. Walter Lowrie (New York: Harper Torchbooks, 1964), is too quirky for an introduction. Better the self-portraying essays in Kaufmann and *The Cambridge Companion to Kierkegaard*, eds. A.S. Hannay and G. Monro (Cambridge: Cambridge University Press, 1998).

Friedrich Nietzsche. Readers should make a start on Heidegger's *Nietzsche*, 2 vols., trans. D.F. Krell (New York: HarperCollins, 1979-84). But for a general overview, there is *The Cambridge Companion to Nietzsche*, eds. B. Magnus and K. Higgins (Cambridge: Cambridge University Press, 1996).

I will add a few general introductory books on Existentialism: J. Macquarrie, *Existentialism* (London: Penguin, 1973); Iris Murdoch, *Existentialists and Mystics*, ed. P. Conradi (London: Penguin, 1999); and the most accessibly pleasant start, George Myerson, *101 Key Ideas: Existentialism*, in the Teach Yourself series (London: Hodder & Stoughton, 2000). George Steiner's *Heidegger*, in the Fontana Modern Masters series (Glasgow: Collins, 1978), is a concise, helpful guide to a difficult philosopher. Iris Murdoch provides a lucid, enjoyable account of *Sartre: The Romantic Rationalist* (London: Penguin, 1989).

The authors

Richard Appignanesi is a writer and editorial director of Icon Books.

Oscar Zarate is a comic-strip artist and illustrator of many of Icon's *Introducing* books. He dedicates this book to his new-born grand-daughter.

Our thanks to Zoran Jevtic for his artwork of the snooker tables.

Photographs, including cover: Judy Groves

Index